The Way It Was
The North Dakota Frontier Experience
Book One: The Sod-busters

Published in the Series

The Way It Was:
The North Dakota Frontier Experience

Coming in 2003

The Way It Was

The North Dakota Frontier Experience
Book One:

The Sod-busters

D. Jerome Tweton and Everett C. Albers, Editors

THE GRASS ROOTS PRESS
Fessenden, North Dakota 58438
Third Printing, 2002

This book is dedicated to the memory of North Dakota pioneers.

Editors: *D. Jerome Tweton and Everett C. Albers*
Designer: *Otto Design of Bismarck, ND*
Printer: *Hignell Book Printing of Winnipeg, Manitoba, Canada*

© 1996 by The Grass Roots Press

PO Box 407
Fessenden, North Dakota 58438-0407

Published by The Grass Roots Press

Printed in Canada

10 9 8 7 6 5 4 3

International Standard Book Number: 0-9650778-0-2 (Book 1)
International Standard Book Number: 0-9650778-1-0 (6-Volume Set)

Library of Congress Catalog Card Number: 95-95347

Table of Contents

Illustrations

First-Person History

D. Jerome Tweton

URING THE GREAT DEPRESSION OF THE 1930s dozens of unemployed North Dakotans kept body and soul together as employees of a unique Federal government project, the Historical Data Project. In 1936, North Dakota's most serious year of drought and depression, the Division of Women's and Professional Projects, a subdivision of the Works Progress Administration (WPA), joined forces with the State Historical Society of North Dakota to interview the state's pioneers and bring together a collection of interviews that would provide future generations with a glimpse at and understanding of life in the 1870s, 1880s, and 1890s.

Interviewers in each county identified the pioneers, interviewed them, and then in some cases typed the interview in story form. Over 5,000 pioneer recollections occupy some forty-two cubic feet as series 529 at the State Historical Society of North Dakota in the Heritage Center, Bismarck. Most of the interviews were conducted in 1937 and 1938, the peak years of project funding. The last biographical notations were completed in early 1941 when the Historical Data Project ended. This is a magnificent collection that provides us with an exceptionally clear window through which to look at the tragedies, trials, and triumphs in the lives of pioneer North Dakotans.

The quality and depth of the interviews vary a great deal, depending upon the ability and energy of the interviewer and the knowledge and memory of the pioneer. Some stories are long and rich in detail; some are short and to the point. Collectively, however, the interviews present a vivid and exciting portrait of what it was like to live in frontier North Dakota. They tell us about "the way it was." For this volume, seventeen individual and family stories have been selected. They present a cross section of geography, life, ethnic backgrounds, and emotional experience. These people and families represent North Dakota's first generation of whites. Their common bond was the sod—that endless sea of grass that challenged the strength and spirit of those who broke it.

The thousands of first-person eyewitness accounts and those in this collection reflect certain themes and experiences that lead us toward a much clearer understanding of our past.

1 Leaving a known life in a known place for an unknown life and in a new land took tremendous courage. A family that struck out from the rugged mountains of Norway, the harsh landscape of Iceland, or the fertile land of southern Russia for a parcel of land in Dakota had a more treacherous and uncertain voyage than did the astronauts who went to the moon. The sea crossing was tough, but no more difficult than the trek from a railhead across an uncharted country to a piece of land that no one else had claimed. More often than not, the land seeker's claim would be staked out twenty to a hundred miles from the railroad.

2 The lure of free or cheap land was terribly powerful. Many people gave up relatively secure lives in other places for a chance to take advantage of the government's appealing land laws. Renting in Wisconsin was no match for owning in Dakota. A little land in Norway was no exchange for a large parcel of land in Dakota. The magnetism of Dakota's land drew not only people who farmed in other places but also a wide assortment of nonfarmers: physicians, factory workers, teachers—even four young Wisconsin women, barely out of their teens. People learned quickly how to use the land laws to their advantage. One could parlay the Preemption Act, the Homestead Act, and the Timber Culture Act (tree claim) into 480 acres. Because the 160-acre preemption cost one dollar, twenty-five cents an acre, the most common combination was a homestead and tree claim for a total of 320 acres. In some cases an unmarried couple would file on adjoining quarters of land and then marry after the land was legally in their hands, providing a 320-acre farm. Family members of legal age worked similar arrangements. In one case a father and his four sons homesteaded adjoining quarters, forming an 800-acre farm. Some land seekers had enough money to buy out a homestead claim or purchase land from a land company or railroad. The draw of North Dakota soil was indeed powerful.

3 Those who came to North Dakota were not failures in nor castoffs from other places. Of course, there were those who ran into business or farm difficulties someplace else and decided to try again in Dakota. These people, however, represented a very small group of the folks who settled in Dakota. The lion's share of those who moved to Dakota came with money in their pockets, the proceeds from the sale of property, a loan from a friend or relative, or savings that had been accumulated through working at this or that job. The Germans from southern Russia, who came by the thousands, left successful farms behind because they did not want to serve in the Russian army and accept Russian ways. The Norwegians, who also came by the thousands, saw Norway as a land with little chance for success so they opted for a greater chance in Dakota. In the 1870s and 1880s many children of successful Illinois, Iowa, and Wisconsin farmers took up land in Dakota because no available land remained at home. Later the same pattern appeared in North Dakota when the children of eastern North Dakota's early settlers took land after 1900 in western North Dakota. A surprising number of people, including physicians, moved to northern Dakota from the East to regain their health in a less humid region.

4 Life was hard. Most farmers barely eked out a living during their first years on the land. The ravages of weather, prairie fires, disease, death, insects, and loneliness took a toll, driving some people away and sapping the energy and spirit of those who stayed. Romanticism has clouded the contemporary view of the "homestead era." Of course, people danced in ten-by-twelve shacks, played cards, and attended quilting bees, but not often. It took several years of backbreaking toil to make a farm go—if indeed it went at all. More often than not, the sod-buster held a second job—perhaps as a farm laborer or a railroad worker or a waitress in a nearby town—in an effort to feed the family or buy seed. Many people did not live in those drafty, quickly built, tarpaper homestead shacks during the first winters, choosing wisely to earn money back home or in town or with an established neighbor. This was not a life for the weak of will or back. It was horribly hard work.

The Way It Was in Photographs

Sod House and Rural Post Office

*Plowing
with oxen
in Dakota*

Heading for the Claim from Williston, North Dakota

At Home on the Prairie

Coffee Break in the Field with the Family

Greeting a Visitor in the Field

Prairie Children at an Early Country School

Taking Time for a Card Game on the Homestead

Reading Between the Lines

Everett C. Albers

In the midst of the toughest of economic times in North Dakota—the 1930s —those hardy pioneers who stayed on in what had become once again an inhospitable place recalled "the way it was" thirty to fifty years past. They spoke with no small pride of what it took to survive "back in the early years."

They survived the blizzards and hail storms, prairie fires and tornadoes. For nearly all who told their stories in this collection, their earliest experience was worse than they imagined. As Charles Kono remembered of his arrival at the immigrant house in Gladstone in 1882, his party of forty "did not act nearly as enthusiastic as we should have on landing in the 'land of plenty'." Terkel Fuglestad's wife remarked upon seeing a sod house, "Look what people have to live in. If we had money, I'd go back home [to Norway] right away." Said Terkel, "And she meant it."

The new home on the Dakota prairie was lonely. Emelia Griepentrog admitted that she had, fifty years before she was interviewed, "cried from dawn to dawn and from dark to dark. I was lonely, afraid to be alone." James Buttree recalled that "My mother, after being on the prairie a month or so, became so lonely that she couldn't endure it. She had come from civilization and found herself in a flat country without a tree, with neighbors sparse and miles away, without means of visiting except walking or ox team, and either mode of traveling meant a desperate battle with mosquitoes."

The further west the claim and the later the time of arrival in Dakota—North Dakota after 1889—the more marginal the chance of a good crop or home improvement. Jacob Kruckenberg came to a homestead just west of the Missouri (actually south) in 1892 after working as a cowboy in the badlands of Teddy Roosevelt fame for three years. Crops were poor, especially wheat. There was national economic depression. He recalls that his parents didn't taste meat for ten months in 1890 on their claim in Mercer County, that they "were hungry and almost without clothes; no money to be made no matter how hard they tried." Yet they persevered. Jacob said that "when we had more money than what we needed for food and clothing, it was saved to build a new lumber house, or barn, as the women did not like to live in the sod shanties without a floor or a piece of furniture."

The earliest photographs of homesteads show that improvements to the tarpaper and/or sod house often came second to a barn of precious lumber. Often, the male partner in a homesteading venture found employment elsewhere while his spouse did most of the work on the farm. In nearly every story in this collection, there is a detailed description of the austerity of the household furniture and the home itself. Between those lines, there is pride in making do with as little as possible.

Terkel Fuglestad became nearly nostalgically romantic in remembering "the way it was": "The future did not look very brightening for them [the homesteaders], but with new courage they started to build homes for themselves and their children on the lone prairie, which hereafter would be their working field. There were many obstacles that came in their way, but the bigger the obstacle, the more interesting it was to overcome it. Such circumstances showed who could stand the test. There was a strife between life and death. It would be a long story if the new settlers were to tell of their experiences from those days about their sacrifices, hopes, disappointments, strife, and victories, but there man and wife stood side by side, enduring the hardships together." Concludes, Fuglestad, who also remembered that his wife was ready to go home, "I have many times thought that the wives of the pioneers should have just as much place in the pages of history as the man."

It was indeed the women—perhaps even more than the men—who found a way to create communities on the northern Great Plains, in spite of all the work and disappointment, the blizzards and hail storms, fire, illness and unfortunate accidents. In the last recollection in this volume, one of the four young women of about twenty years who came to the northwestern corner of North Dakota in 1900 said they came because "An idea struck me. What fun it would be." Sally Troska remembered blizzards as the best of times that she, her sister Mary, and cousins Helen and Christina Sonnek had during their proving-up period in Dakota. It was a time when homesteaders found themselves thrown together in close quarters—in one instance, she and her cousin Christina spent four days snowed in with an eighty-two-year-old widow and her three bachelor sons. The teenage woman homesteader and her sister baked for the "old mother" whose hair, Mary remembered, "was burned off of her head from the result of putting kerosene in the boiler with soap."

The careful reader will find between the lines of the stories of these early Dakota pioneers the conclusion that cooperation and hospitality were critical to survival. Visitors are always welcome, including the native Indian people who stop in for a meal. Among the most remarkable of memories in this collection is Paulina Schueter's tale of taking acorns from those gathered in hollow branches by squirrels: "We took about half of the acorns from the tree, and then decided that we hadn't better steal any more because we would leave the squirrels without any food for the winter."

The acorns were shared by Pauline's family, who used them as a substitute for coffee; by the family hog; and by the squirrels who gathered them. In fact, neighborliness appears in nearly every story; there are but two or three references to theft or any aggressive behavior. Even Jesse James and his brother Frank are the most gentlemanly of guests at a homesteader's shack.

About the editing . . .

The words are those of the pioneers. Most of the stories were recorded in the third-person by WPA workers. Those collected in this volume have been changed to first-person narratives. There have been punctuation and grammatical changes as well as the occasional insertion of words for the sake of clarity.

From Switzerland To Dakota

Agatha Jerel Arms

The rain came in torrents and the hail in chunks, some as large as a good-sized coconut.

Agatha was born to Andrew and Agnes Jerel in 1856. The Jerels operated a small but diversified farm: vegetables, grain, fruit, sheep, and cows. Agatha attended public school until she was fifteen. In 1870 her mother died suddenly. Her father experienced uncontrollable grief and could not even think of remaining on the farm that he had shared for so many years with his wife. In 1871 he sold his farm and took his children to the United States which he called "the land of plenty." He developed a successful farm near Alma, Wisconsin. Sometime in the late 1870s Agatha met Lorenz Arms who was working with his brother, Thomas, on their uncle's not-too-distant dairy farm. In 1882 the Arms brothers left Wisconsin for Dakota Territory where Lorenz homesteaded near Wimbledon. The next year he returned to Wisconsin to marry Agatha. She, like many young women, made the journey to Dakota after a fiancé or husband had established the farm.

I N THE SPRING OF 1871 father with his two sons and daughters took only personal belongings and embarked from Braatz, Switzerland, on a steam boat called *Homonia* which came from Hamburg, Germany.

I was fifteen and recall the awful seasickness of the passengers on the boat. I was lucky, however, and wasn't bothered at all. My brothers were sick the first two days; but they got used to it, and after a few days weren't bothered any more. One lady became sick and died on the boat. They dropped her in the ocean. I thought that was terrible at first, but later when I heard that the sharks would tip the boat over if they didn't drop the body overboard, I felt different.

There were times of great excitement and fear on the trip. One night the *Homonia* met another much larger than she. The captain on the larger boat had blown a whistle warning another ship, but for some unknown reason the captain on the *Homonia* didn't hear the whistle. About five minutes later the captains were talking to each other from the boats side by side. The next morning it was rumored that if the *Homonia* had been struck by the larger boat, they would have all perished.

A few nights later the boiler on the *Homonia* broke. Everyone was very excited and filled with fear. The ship stopped for repair for two days. Some of the passengers were afraid the boiler wouldn't be fixed; others were afraid of the sharks, and some that their food would run short while they were stalled. On the morning of the third day the ship sailed again.

The *Homonia* landed in New York harbor on May 2, 1871, eleven days after leaving Braatz. We Jerels went directly to Castle Garden where our trunks were examined. Here we spent one night. The next day we left by train for Wisconsin. We had to stop at Chicago on Saturday night and stay over until Sunday to make train connections.

After supper we all went for a ride and drove around Chicago to see the ruins of the big fire. Along the lake, the roads had a foundation of boards because the water would come up in gushes and wash the dirt away. As we drove around, we could see where these roads were a total ruin because the fire burned the wood that supported them. This fire of 1871 swept a large territory and was very destructive.

The next day we took a train bound for Alma, Wisconsin. Upon arriving at Alma, father hired a man with a team and a wagon to take our trunks to a rooming house. Here we stayed for one week while father was out looking for a small farm. The following week he found one, and we moved out there. I was busy getting settled, preparing meals, and doing the little tasks a mother usually has to do. I was very happy and content. Father, Ruben, and Tom were busy buying stock and machinery. [The Jerels, except for Agatha, remained in Wisconsin.]

My friendship with Lorenz Arms ripened into love, and on March 4, 1883, in the presence of relatives and intimate friends we were married in the little Eagle Valley church. After the ceremony the neighbors gave a big wedding dinner for us. I received many gifts, but probably the most welcome was a cow and a team of horses, gifts from father and my brothers.

The following Monday we left by train for our new home near Wimbledon [twenty-five miles northeast of Jamestown]. The stock was shipped in a box car. When we reached the station, Lorenz's brother Tom was waiting. We unloaded the stock and started for the homestead. There was only a little one-room frame building and a sod barn on the place. The furniture was very crude—the chairs were covered nail kegs. Lorenz filed on his homestead in 1881. His brother filed on a homestead in 1881, too.

In the year of 1886 the crop looked fine, but just as the wheat was in the dough, there was a killing frost which froze thousands of acres of splendid grain. Fields that looked fine and full of life were lifeless the next day. Harvesting was on; women helped in the field; everyone did his share to save every bushel of grain. When it was threshed it was light, shrunken, and shriveled. Some of it was saved for seed, some for flour, but the most of it was used for feed. Here and there were fields that the frost had missed so that the crop was not a total loss.

The winter of 1889 was a severe one. There were many cold days and bad storms, including a real blizzard. One morning the sun was shining, but it was twenty or twenty-five degrees below zero. Just before noon everything seemed to change; the air turned hazy and smoky; the sun disappeared from out of sight; and before anyone realized what had happened the storm was here. My husband had gone to Wimbledon after a load of coal and was half way home when the storm started. He knew too well an old-fashioned blizzard was approaching. Driving into a farm, he unhitched his team and put them in the barn. Being greatly worried over me who was home alone, he started on foot across the field. The storm grew worse, and facing that terrific wind that was coming directly from the north made matters all the worse. Lorenz hurried, but it was hard plowing through the snow. He was growing very

3

stiff and cold; the fine powdery snow was switching in his eyes, nose, and mouth. He was sure he was going the right direction and kept on plowing through drift after drift. One time he fell; but, staggering, he lifted himself up and was on his way. Glancing across the field, he could see a little light which he followed for about a mile. Soon he came closer and closer and hazily saw a house. He walked to the door and pounded; the door flew open, and he fell to the floor. When he woke up, he was lying on a bed, not in his own home but exactly ten miles north of the farm. Several people froze to death during that blizzard. Many bodies were not found until the snow melted in the spring.

One day in July 1905, the temperature was very high and the air seemed to be charged with heat, but in the afternoon a decided change was noticeable. Light breezes sprung up and about four o'clock it was considerably cooler. Many clouds were gathering in the northwest; they gradually grew larger and seemed to be coming nearer. They were of various colors, some light and fleecy, some dark and fierce, and others a golden color. Then in just a few minutes the breeze died down, and the whole sky turned black; the clouds were one solid blaze of electricity. The terrific peals of thunder seemed to shake the ground; the wind came up in gushers, and the air was filled with dust and dirt. Boxes, boards, and tin were flying here and there. Then came the rain and hail. The rain came in torrents and the hail in chunks, some as large as a good-sized coconut. The ground was covered to a depth of three inches with hail. The storm lasted about ten minutes, and, from four to six miles wide, destroyed everything in its path. All the light frame buildings and many of the larger ones were a total wreck. Gardens were plastered and grain fields were bare and black. Our 120 acres of wheat on a tree claim would have yielded two thousand bushels, but it was all hailed out. This storm was the most destructive and covered the largest area of any hail storm we had ever witnessed.

On A Tree Claim Near Guelph

The Batemans

The doctor said, "There is no use to doctor if you care to live; a change of climate might help you."

As did many early settlers, the Batemans moved to Dakota upon the recommendation of their physician. William Bateman, a native of Michigan, took a tree claim in 1881, not far from Guelph, near what would become the North Dakota-South Dakota border. He followed the familiar pattern of preceding his family in order to work the claim and build a house. Mrs. Bateman joined him the following year. He also, like many settlers, supplemented his meager farm income with other employment—in his case, teaching. Bateman eventually quit farming and went into the hotel business in Ludden, Hecla, Lebanon, and Eureka, South Dakota. He later owned the Argyl Hotel in Oakes which became the Bateman's permanent residence. Mrs. Bateman recalls the early years around Guelph.

M Y HUSBAND AND I EACH HAD POOR HEALTH, and the doctor said: "There is no use to doctor if you care to live; a change of climate might help you." So my husband decided to come to Dakota and his younger brother, Chester, decided to accompany him.

They left Mason, Michigan, on April 1, 1881. Upon arrival in Dakota, they settled on a tree claim located one mile from Guelph. For six weeks thereafter William's cough seemed to grow worse, then began to change for the better.

They remained in Dakota until Christmas that year and did carpenter work and farm work for themselves and others. They helped to build many houses and a blacksmith shop and to install scales and signs. However, they worked on their own claims much of the time and cooked their own meals in the little shanties.

After returning to Michigan at Christmas time, they began to make plans for returning to Dakota. In April 1882 they chartered two cars and loaded them with the various articles and stock which they were going to need—lumber for William's house; complete household goods consisting of kitchen chairs, rockers, two beds, carpet, table, and everything in the line of dishes; and a No. 7 cook stove, melodeon, tool chest and set of carpenter tools; a cow, chickens, ducks, a two-gallon crock of butter and the same of lard, and some farm tools. All of these arrived safely at their destination. They obtained teams and hauled the lumber and supplies to their claims. Their first team was oxen for which they paid $150, but they soon had horses for working and for driving with the buggy. It was sixteen miles to Ellendale, where we obtained groceries. Oakes was also sixteen miles distant.

When my husband returned to Dakota the second time, he was accompanied by his brothers—Dudley, Thomas, and Calvin. Dudley took a claim near Frederick, South Dakota. Chester's claim was located two and one-half miles northeast from our claim. Chester's, Calvin's and Thomas' claims joined so that at the table in their shanty they each sat on his own claim.

Soon the eighteen- by twenty-four-foot house, including bedroom and kitchen, was completed, and my husband wrote for me to come. I left Michigan on August 28, 1882, with our little daughter, Mabel, age four years, two months. During the course of my journey, I heard men talking on the train, saying that the dirt blew so terribly in Dakota that it was impossible to tell whether men were white or black. When my husband met my train, he walked by me and went the length of the car and came back without my recognizing him. It was not until he spoke to me that I knew who he was; he had been threshing all day at Frederick and had had no opportunity to clean up.

The next day was Saturday. In the morning one of my brothers-in-law came to town to get us. We left Ellendale after dinner and went to Calvin's claim, where two sisters of his wife, Tilly and Mattie Hillman, lived. They each had a shanty where they slept on the land on which they had filed. The cooking and eating were done in a cookhouse which was located on the corners of the claims. The table was arranged so that each was sitting on his own land while eating. On our trip to this locality we saw places in the ground where they said buffalo stampedes had passed, and we also passed through a cloud of flying ants. The road seemed very long. The sky was dark with clouds which threatened rain, but they soon passed away. The girls had a good supper; and after the dishes were washed, each went to his own shanty to sleep.

The following morning we soon were on our way because I was anxious to see our new home. Upon arrival, I found my new little house filled up with a long work bench and shavings all over the floor. A line strung across the room was loaded with quilts, pillows, feather bed and clothing. It did not take me long to clear this out. We raised a garden and, as we had plenty of groceries, we did not fare badly. All our water we took from a slough until a well was dug and curbed up. We built a barn in the side of the hill for stock and hay.

On December 4, 1888, my birthday, a big fire came. My husband said not to go out of doors and not to let Mabel out. He took gunny sacks, wet them in the slough which was close to the barn, and fought the fire. The fresh dirt which had been thrown out when the cellar was dug also helped to turn the fire aside. The fire went on either side of the barn and other buildings and swept on.

We had many blizzards and much deep snow and cold weather. We longed for summer to come, although we also had summer storms with much heavy thunder and sharp lightning. Sometimes crops were destroyed when the fields of promising grain were swept as clean as though the seed had never been planted.

Two preachers from Oakes often visited us and stayed with us overnight. Neighbors also often gathered at our house for a pleasant time. We played such games as drop the handkerchief and rolled platter. One neighbor had a marble slab which he had brought with him, and we made candy for all. Sometimes when they came for an evening, a bad blizzard would come up and they would have to stay all night.

Guelph in the Early Years

Still, with all of the hard times, we had much to be thankful for.

My husband was township clerk for a number of years; the meetings were held at our home. Since there was no other place to get meals, I served free food to as many as twelve men at some of these all-day meetings. Mr. Bateman was also a school teacher; he had taught in Michigan before coming to Dakota. He was a Mason and an Odd Fellow. He endured many hardships of pioneer life in helping to blaze the trail for the later settlers. When he gave up teaching, I boarded the teachers.

My brother Frank came to Dakota at age sixteen. He walked the sixteen miles from Ellendale to our farm. He came back to Dakota with Chester Bateman who had been back to Michigan for a visit in March 1883. My mother came to Dakota in the fall of 1884. She was a widow—my father died in 1883. She took up [purchased] a homestead, for which she paid $250. She had three boys to care for. My sister also came later.

In 1886 the railroad was built past our home to Ellendale, and I boarded nine of the men while they were laying the track near our place. A station, bank buildings and stores were built at Guelph.

The Quebec Love Birds

Ludger and Albina Berard

Her mother would watch us through the crack of the door to see that nothing was said or done out of place.

Both Ludger and Albina came as children to Dakota from the Province of Quebec, Canada. She lived in St. Lin, a little town near Montreal, where her father earned a meager living. A Mr. Geroux, whom her father knew well, urged him to take advantage of the rich farmland that was available around Pembina. On March 15, 1880, the family left St. Lin for Pembina country. Ludger's father farmed "one hundred acres of tall timber" about one hundred miles from Montreal. In 1871 the family moved to Massachusetts where family members found work in a factory. In 1874 they joined "the great push" to Rhode Island where they worked in factories for six years. Here Ludger worked with Frank Hebert who later moved to the Pembina area and played a key role in the Berard family sojourn to Dakota. In 1880 the Berards moved once again, back to their tall timber near Montreal. The Dakota story began in 1884.

Ludger's Story:

I ALWAYS HEARD FROM FRANK HEBERT and knew where he was and what he was doing. So in 1880 he wanted us to come to Dakota Territory, but my father wanted to go back to Canada since he had that timber farm. So back we went and stayed there until March 17, 1884. So my people left Canada by passenger train, crossing over into the United States at Port Huron, Michigan. From there we took another train on to Hamilton, Dakota Territory. We landed in Hamilton on March 23, 1884. Frank Hebert was there to meet us with a team and sleigh. All that we had brought with us was our bedding and personal things. We had all this packed into boxes and trunks.

We stayed with the Hebert family for a month, and then we rented a log house [in Hamilton]. We paid five dollars a month for that house. It was very small, but we lived in it until the first of June. During our stay in this log shack, my father located some land near Pembina. This land was taken, but the man named Quinnell wanted to sell his home-stead right to my father. Mr. Quinnell wanted $1,700, which included all the machinery, horses, oxen, household goods, and buildings on the farm. So after the first of June we moved to our home about eight miles west of Pembina.

That first spring when we came, I rented forty acres of land from Lizzie Hebert, a sister of Frank Hebert. I bought a team of oxen for $175. With this team I put in the crop on those forty acres. This farm was two miles north from Cavalier. I had a very good crop of wheat on this farm; I raised about twenty bushels to the acre. I hauled it all to Hamilton and sold it for fifty cents per bushel. I remember when I was hauling my wheat to Hamilton that I would see a farmer come all the distance from Olga with a load of wheat in sacks—all that the oxen could pull. Wheat was always hauled in sacks in the early days. I used to feel sorry for the farmers who lived up in Cavalier County because it took them three days to make the trip with their oxen, and then when the grain was frozen, the price was less, so sometimes they just broke even. It cost them to stay all night and take care of their team. I used to think how lucky we were that we lived in Pembina County since the frost never hit us very much.

After that first year of farming for myself, I went to help my father farm his land. Then in the fall of 1887 I bought a homesteader's right from a man named Sargent for $400. This also included a small log shack about fourteen by twenty which had one room upstairs and one room downstairs; all the furniture was in the house, too. Of course, the furniture wasn't much—only a baby's high chair, an old low cook stove, a homemade table, and a couple of old kitchen chairs. This was the home I had for my wife when I got married.

A Pioneer Log Cabin in the Red River Valley

Before I tell you of my wedding, I want to tell you how we courted in those olden days. I well remember when I went to see my wife, we sat downstairs in a room off the kitchen that was used for the dining and sitting room. Her mother would watch us through the crack of the door to see that nothing was said or done out of place. Sometimes the family would go upstairs to bed, but her mother didn't go to bed. She would watch through the cracks of the floor to see that all was well. The upstairs floors in those log shacks were nailed with cracks in between the boards of about one-half inch to let the heat go upstairs to warm up the room. So these cracks proved to be very handy if the daughter had a beau. I was always watched until I went home, and that was by ten or earlier as I knew better than to stay any longer. When I decided to go home, I would try and watch my chance and say goodbye with a handshake so her mother wouldn't see it. That was the only way we could show our affection.

We were married in the Catholic church in Pembina, about ten o'clock in the morning one Sunday by Father Gutra. The priest lived in Emerson, Manitoba, and came only every two weeks to Pembina to say mass. So all that wanted to get married always had to do so on Sundays because he could not come any other time. My wife's parents served the dinner, and my folks served the supper; only the relatives were at the dinner and supper, but at the church it was public for all. We never had a honeymoon, never heard of a honeymoon in those days. We stayed all night at my father's place, and the next day we moved over to my little log shack. It was very dirty so we papered it with newspapers which made it nice and clean; so every time it was dirty, we did the same thing over again. It was papered like this for ten years, the whole time we lived in it. This one hundred and sixty acres had only twelve acres broke. I owned no machinery so my father would let me use his, and when I could afford it, I bought my own.

Most everyone seeded their crops by hand, but my father had a gatlin gun seeder, so I used to seed mine with it too. This seeder was placed in the rear of a wagon; a chain from the seeder was attached to the hub of the rear wagon wheel; an apparatus with cogs was around the hub very tight so when the chain was in place and the team started to go, it drove the fans in the seeder, and the faster the team pulled the wagon, the faster and the farther the grain would go broadcast. The seeder had a large hopper, and in this hopper the grain was poured from sacks that were in the front of the wagon. This was by far faster than by hand and every one thought, "what an invention." Our crops were all very good; so were the gardens. The land was so rich that we didn't need the rain like we do today [1938].

I didn't have much of an education in my days. I only had English school through the third grade, and then before we left Quebec to come to Dakota Territory, my father sent us boys for nine months to a French convent. During these nine months I learned simple reading. So in order to keep up our French, father subscribed for a French paper called *La Press* which was printed in Montreal. When I got married, I subscribed for it myself as I had gotten to read so well I really missed my French paper after I left home.

W Albina's Story:

E MADE THE TRIP IN FIVE DAYS. We had our own eats with us and could only have hot tea on the trip. Hot water was always ready for us. L. Geroux was there to meet us, and he took us to Westline, a mile southwest of Emerson where the custom

The 1863 home of the first home-steader in northern Dakota, Charles Cavileer of Pembina

house is located. Here we had to stay all night because we had to report, and then the river was so high that we needed daylight to go across. We stayed at the custom house and had one large room; here we all put what few blankets we had on the floor and rested the best we could. Our bedding did not come the same time we did, so we were very short of bedding. The next morning we got a row boat and started to cross the Red River. The edge of the river was all water, so we rowed the boat until we hit ice and then we picked up our boat and walked until we came to the water on the other side, and then we rowed again.

We stayed with L. Geroux for about a week, and then my father bought a homestead right from Louis Rolette (son of Joe Rolette); he paid $500 for it, and all that was on the place was a log shack and that didn't amount to much. This shack was about eleven by eighteen with a straw and mud mixture put over logs; the floor was made from elm bark. This bark was skinned from the trees when green and then laid down flat to dry; when dry it is ready to lay down as a floor. This floor was very rough and needed no scrubbing. There was a log floor laid on about half of the building for the upstairs, and here we put a load of straw and the boys just crawled into this straw like a bunch of hogs. You could see them from below. They got up to their sleeping quarters by using a ladder, and when father needed the ladder outside for anything, he just came in and got it. There was a bed in the shack and father put boards across the springs and laid a big pile of straw on this for him and mother to sleep on. We didn't have our bedding yet because of high water, so some of the neighbors gave us what they could spare, but still in the month of April you needed a lot of covers, so we just crawled under the straw. We slept like this for about two weeks until the water went down. In the meantime two of my brothers took a cold and died from this way of living. After two months my father bought lumber and put in a real floor. We had a very small, low four-hole cook stove. We got all our fuel from our own land so we could burn all the wood we needed to keep warm.

Wild strawberries and raspberries were plentiful in those early days. I remember when I was about ten or eleven years old I went with my brothers and sisters to pick them. We waded through water up to our waist many times until we crossed the marsh, and then we walked to where the berries were about a mile and a half from Pembina. We each took a gallon pail, and we picked these full and then walked to Pembina and sold them at one dollar per gallon, and when the raspberries were ripe, we did the same thing and got eighty cents per gallon. That first summer we children made over eight dollars and every summer we picked berries for several years.

When we first came we had no chickens, and they were scarce and could not be bought so we children would look for all kinds of wild eggs—duck, prairie chicken, goose, mud hen, snipe, and crane. We used to cook and bake with them and were glad to get them. The Indians did the same. And many times we found eggs that were partly started to hatch, and the Indians always wanted them; at first we thought they were going to set them and have them hatch, but that was not the case. They boiled them and ate them as food. When the Indians cooked any kind of fowl, they never cleaned them at all. Just take the entrails out and then hang the fowl over the fire, and when it's done, the feathers peel off very easily. I remember that the Indians came many times and asked for our white bread, and at first we didn't know what they wanted so they just came in the house and would point to the white bread.

Meeting Up With Jesse and Frank James

James Buttree

We are brothers; our name is James.

In 1879 James Buttree's older brother, John, preempted a quarter section of land south of Grand Forks. His positive reports prompted the rest of the family to join him from their home in Peterboro, Ontario, where George, the father, worked in a sawmill. The senior Buttree caught Dakota fever and the next year was situated on a preemption claim south of Grand Forks. The family increased the territorial population by eleven. James Buttree, who was born in 1869, recalls those dynamic years in the Red River Valley. The family built a house in Grand Forks in 1881 and lived there during the winters so that the children could attend public school. Although James had chores on his father's farm, he also worked for the Grand Forks Herald *and the* Plaindealer *during the 1880s. He became interested in the machinery aspect of farming and in 1901 moved to Valley City where he formed an implement company partnership and later owned an automobile dealership. He remained a life-long bachelor.*

WE ARRIVED THERE [the quarter south of Grand Forks] during the early afternoon. The man fed his horses, and mother served a lunch and a "cup of tea"; being Canadians, we didn't know what coffee was. The man then hitched up and drove away to return to Grand Forks. It was then that we had our first experience with the loneliness of the prairies and the wildness of it all. Alone on that flat landscape, and as evening came on, the mosquitoes made their presence known, and we had no mosquito screen; we had not thought of that. We had to close the windows and live through the evening without ventilation and annoyed by the mosquitoes that had already entered. There were two beds in one end of the shanty, nailed to the walls; the walls formed one side and one end of each bedstead—homemade bedsteads, of course. There was a homemade table, a few plain chairs, one rocking chair, a stove, and some homemade shelves for dishes nailed to the wall. We retired with the darkness that first night on the prairie to escape the loneliness in sleep.

We were awakened early the next morning by meadowlarks singing on the roof. We got up and had some tea and something to eat. The day was beautiful but lonely. A short distance from the shanty was a slough, and it was well populated with wild life. The wild feathered folk talked continuously that day, which added to the wildness, yet detracted from the loneliness. It was truly "a quack-quack here and a quack-quack there, here a quack and there a quack and everywhere a quack-quack," and the same almost of the "honk-honks." As night approached that second evening, we scanned the horizon, anticipating the arrival of a yoke of oxen and wagon. Finally it came into view. How good it looked, because it meant the arrival of father and brother Will. They arrived about dark, and oh, the mosquitoes they brought with them. We made a smudge for the oxen and placed it so that its smoke rested over the shanty. The load consisted of a half-barrel of salt pork, a keg of syrup, flour, and other food stuffs, and a peacemaker breaking plow. The presence of father and Will brought relief from the loneliness, and the shanty began to take on a comfy feeling.

The following day saw the first operations in breaking up the prairie sod. Father and Will rigged up the plow and hitched the oxen to it. There was no difficulty except that there should have been three oxen instead of two, but consideration was used in that respect. On that first day of plowing Fred and I were initiated into the art of farm labor in the new homeland by picking buffalo bones out of the way of the breaking plow.

One field of wheat, another of oats, and some potatoes were planted. The oats were an excellent crop as were the potatoes, which were planted by dropping sets behind the plow in every third furrow. Father had his doubts about planting potatoes in that manner; however, there was plenty of moisture that summer, and a most excellent crop of early rose and peachblow potatoes was realized. The wheat was planted on lower ground and was very disappointing; very little grew.

The storms that swept the prairies that summer seemed to be very violent indeed. I really believe they were worse that season than they have ever been since that time. A shanty of one room built of one thickness of shiplap lumber makes an ideal sounding board when hailstones of large dimensions begin a bombardment. The tarpaper on the roof didn't last longer than the first shot; therefore, every hail storm meant a deluge. My mother, after being on the prairie a month or so, became so lonely that she couldn't endure it. She had come from civilization and found herself in a flat country without a tree, with neighbors sparse and miles away, without means of visiting except walking or ox team, and either mode of traveling meant a desperate battle with mosquitoes. The music (racket would be a better term) of the wild birds was constant. The cry of the snipe was persistent; it was a weird sound without melody. Wild ducks quacked only a few rods from our door. The wild goose honked, and the sand hill crane a mile in the sky sounded a tremulous baritone. The plover's mournful wail as it alights from a flight (and they were continuously alighting) and the meadowlark's song on our shanty roof before sunrise not only became tiresome but prevented natural rest. The wildness of it all was distracting to a woman used to the conventionalities of civilization. So one day father yoked the oxen, and he and mother went to town where she visited a daughter who lived there. As they moved away over the prairie in the brand new Jackson wagon toward the distant city, fourteen miles away, we kiddies were instructed to go to an aunt who had just arrived on the prairie and was living in a little homesteader's shack while her larger shanty was under construction. That was an awful night. A storm came from the west; the hail was terrific, the rain came in torrents, the wind a hurricane. How that little shack hung to its foundations is a conundrum. The hail cut the tarpaper on the roof, and the water came through in a shower until it couldn't get away through the cracks between the floor boards as rapidly as it came in, and the floor was a lake. The beds were soaked. They were improvised beds on the floor, and they were in the water. No matter where one stood, it was impossible to find a dry place. The hail stones pounded the thin walls until it was almost impossible to make each other heard by shouting. The wind howled, and the lightning flashed constantly while the thunder pealed a terrific cannonade. A mile away our neighbor in a more secure household sat in his window with a large field glass, and the continuous lightning enabled him to find us, and he watched us throughout the storm to ascertain if we survived safely.

That summer was spent in constructive play except when I was picking buffalo bones out of the way of the breaking plow. My younger brother and I built railroads through the alkali beds where the grass didn't grow. We saw the work of the builders as the railroad was constructed westward, so we made miniature railroads. We got some sheet iron spools from a neighbor who had a wire binder, and with those spools we manufactured cars. Instead of rails we had creases or grooves in the roadbed which the wheels followed. Our railroad had depots, sidings, and a turntable. We even built a hearse with which to conduct the funeral rites of dead gophers. Several gophers received a solemn burial after a tedious journey to the cemetery. Some of these gophers died in our well. Our well was a kind of community affair—gophers, toads, frogs, and mice persisted in getting into it—and gophers and mice couldn't live in it. The reason we didn't have a good well was that there was no good water. Father did much laborious work sinking in different places in search of good water. Finally he succeeded, and then we had a real well properly stoned to the top. Up to that time (September) we were compelled to live on water that was inhabited by frogs and toads, gophers, and mice, water which was intensely alkali. It is well that it isn't what goeth in at the mouth that defileth a man.

I have only mentioned one of the awful nights of that first summer, but there were many strenuous times during that period; times that caused much wear and tear to the nervous system. During the fall of that year there was a smoke in the west for days, getting greater and greater, and during the nights the western horizon was a great flame of red. At last it came one Sunday morning and swept by us. Our shanty was protected by firebreaks—first, second, and third lines of defense, as it were. We had faith in our defenses, but the onslaught was a horrible sight to behold. It swept by with its smoke and heat and left us safe but on a changed landscape. We were now inhabitants of a great black sea.

One Sunday during September 1880, two gentlemen on horseback rode up to our shanty. They came direct across country from the east and not via the Fort Totten trail. They were mounted on beautiful bay horses of 1,100 or 1,200 weight. They asked if they might rest and feed their horses and get some dinner. Of course, we were delighted to have them with us; strangers were always welcome, more than welcome; their presence was always a diversion from the monotony of being so much alone. They dismounted, led their horses to the shady side of the shanty where they removed the saddles, saddle blankets, and other parapher-nalia. They had double-barrel shot guns of the muzzle-loading type of that day lashed to their saddles along with blankets, oats in sacks for the horses, and iron sugar stakes with lariats for staking the horses out to grass. These men were quite picturesque in appearance. They were dressed exactly alike: brown-striped trousers, tucked into high top boots, were supported by heavy leather belts; each belt had two holsters carrying old style Colt 44 revolvers. The guns were worn in front with butts to center; or, the cross-arm draw, and not at the hips as is customary with the modern stage villain. And, I might say that when guns were considered, not much escapes the attention of the small boy. They wore blue flannel shirts laced in front and loosely tied black sailor ties, black slouch hats. They had coats, but I do not have a clear recollection of their coats.

After staking out their horses and feeding them, they came to the shanty. As they stepped in and shook hands, they held back their identification, waiting for father to move first. Father said, "We are Canadians. We came out from Ontario in the spring." The taller of the two then stated, "We are brothers; our name is James; we live in Missouri near Kansas City." Mother responded first. After all the years I can hear mother saying, "Oh, from Missouri; I have never met people from that far south before."

The reason for Frank James' (I learned his given name later) waiting for father to announce himself first was to learn our geographi-cal environment before coming to Dakota. Had father said, "We came from Goodhue County, Minnesota in the spring," Frank would have said something like this: "My name is Woodson; this gentleman is Mr.

Howard," and their home might have been given as Timbuctoo. But Ontario having been mentioned, he knew we had never heard of them because facilities for gathering news and disseminating it were very crude then compared

Jesse (left) and Frank (right) James in the 1870s

to today. So he boldly told us the truth, and we were none the wiser.

A very interesting conversation was carried on during dinner by father, mother, and Frank. Mother thought Frank James was a very interesting young man; he had such a fund of information as well as being a fluent conversationalist. My memory of this visit is very exact not only because of the guns and general picturesqueness of the men, but Fred and I had to wait for dinner. Frank was about five-foot eleven and slender with long features, an aquiline nose, and a light mustache; he carried his head slightly forward. Jesse was an inch or two shorter, stoutly built; he stood very erect and wore a heavy brown beard.

Shortly after dinner they saddled their horses and led them to the door before taking leave. They offered to pay for their entertainment, but their thanks were accepted instead. After some more visiting while parting, they shook hands with father, mother, and Will—Fred and I were considered small fry. Frank did all the talking and most of the smiling and laughing. Jesse was a stoic. His only speech was when he shook hands and said, "Good bye." They mounted their horses and rode away to the west.

A Long Pull From Stavanger

Terkel Fuglestad

"Look what people have to live in. If we had money, I'd go back home right away." And she meant it.

Terkel Fuglestad was born in 1856 at Bjerkrean, Sogn, Fjeld-bygd, a mountain town on the west coast of Norway. His family ran a farm of fourteen cows and sixty sheep. When he was eighteen, he attended the military school at Kristiana. In 1880 he married Abigal Osland, also from Bjerkrean. With no prospect of acquiring the family's farm or of finding employment in a depressed Norwegian economy, the young Norwegian couple struck out for the prairies of Dakota. His story is the common one of most Dakota homesteads: little money and hard work.

I N 1883 MY WIFE ABIGAL AND I packed our clothes and set sail for America. In all these years it has not been with my good will that I am here, but it was God's will, and so it was for the best. There is a feeling of satisfaction and peace to know that you are led by God's Almighty hand.

There was an economic crisis in Stavanger, Norway, in the beginning of the eighties. I wouldn't overtake my father's farm as he wanted me to, so we moved to town and tried to get some kind of office work, but wherever I went, it seemed they were more than filled up. At last I got work at a foundry and shipyard where steamships were being built. Then one day they laid off one hundred men, and I was among the unlucky. After that it seemed as though all ways for work were closed.

The only way was to set my course westward across the ocean.

I had often talked to Halvor Nordaas, who was the manager of the fire department and was city gardener in Stavanger, about getting a job as city gardener. Just as I was ready to go to America, I got word I could have the job. If I had known it sooner, I would not be here now. Planting of trees and flowers has always been my dearest work; so goodbye, Norway, and I left for the strange country of the Dakota prairies.

After fourteen days on the steamship from Rotterdam, Holland, we arrived in New York. We hadn't been ashore two hours when I got the biggest surprise I ever had since I set my feet on American soil. The immigrants were gathered in a large six-cornered room where benches were fastened to the wall. Most of them stood in groups around the room. After living two weeks on spoiled vegetables and half-fried biscuits, we were near starved. I had bought a loaf of rye bread and had a little butter left from Norway. We sat on the bench with our backs to the wall and ate. The bread lay on the bench between us. I was going to cut myself another slice when to my surprise the bread was gone. We jumped up and looked around, but the bread was stolen right out of our hands. Of course, the thief was in one of the other groups looking at us. My wife has always been a hard worker and soon forgot about it and took her knitting and needles and started to knit. She laid a large ball of wool yarn by her side on the bench. All of a sudden the end of the thread was in her hands. The ball of yarn had also been stolen. I soon came to the conclusion that the thief was a careless woman who continued walking back and forth conversing in Norwegian to the people. She sat and talked to my wife and later followed us to the restaurant to purchase some coffee. This was a warning of what I could expect in the new land.

Our route went through the Great Lakes from Buffalo to Duluth and took about a week. We traveled as freight goods. We had our bedding with, and at night we made our bed under deck among piles of freight goods. On the other side of the deck were fourteen milk cows in rows. We were a flock of Finlanders, three Norwegians, and one Swede. Several times we had to move our bedding when the goods was to be taken or assessed. So as not to be in the way, the Swede had made his bed on top of a pile of goods.

After a month's journey, we reached Valley City, Dakota Territory. There I met my brother-in-law, E. Aarestad. The next day we followed the train as far as the rails were built, two miles north of the present Hannaford. You will note Mrs. Aarestad and her two small boys were in our company to Dakota—Mr. Aarestad had come the year previous.

We unloaded the provisions on the prairie near the Hetland farm where some men were working on the rails. One of them, Matius Johnson, had oxen with and drove us two miles to Aarestad's homestead. At last we came to our destination where our future home was to be.

I hadn't been on the Dakota prairies very long before I felt the urge to hunt. I had taken with me from Norway a small gun, and not far from Jens Bull's place there was a pond where ducks were floating around. There was high grass around, and all of a sudden I saw a pretty animal with a bush tail and white stripes on its back. I ran after it but very soon had to retrace my steps. The air was full of a choking smell. It followed along with me. I had barely stepped inside the door when I heard the cry "Out! Out!" They threw some clothes out to me and ordered me to bury the clothes I had on. This was a new adventure for me. In my childhood days I had read in *Nature's History* of the *stenkdynet* (skunk) on the American prairies. It now became more clear to me, having experienced it. What did we think of America? Oh, we thought it quite interesting and romantic and felt at home. And my wife? Yes, it was just one time she lost her courage in all these years following my hunting experience. I came and there she stood, looking very downcast. She pointed to the sod house and said, "Look what people have to live in. If we had money, I'd go back home right away." And she meant it. She came from a rich home in Norway where there was luxury, not making this very inviting. But then we visited some neighbors down by the Sheyenne River, and there she met some acquaintances from her neighborhood in Norway. These neighbors had been here about two years and had things quite comfortable. Her courage returned and from then on she has been quite satisfied.

I took my homestead three days after I came to Dakota. Elling Johnson (Froiland) and Jens Bull had filed on the same section earlier in the summer. They told me the southwest quarter of the section (where a shanty was) had not been filed on and told me I could go to Cooperstown and get papers on it. I had Jens Bull's ten-year-old daughter to go with me to Cooperstown and be my interpreter. They asked me what section it was; but I didn't know it. Then this little girl said, "It's section ten we live on." The men soon found out the rest.

My three brothers had come to America two years previous. I had received a letter from my oldest brother that if I came to America, I should bring some *merskums* (smoking pipes) because they were so expensive in America. I then bought the finest pipe I could find in Stavanger, with a long stem and pearl band, for speculation.

I now had to build a house on my homestead. Elling Johnson urged me to go to Cooperstown and buy a shanty which stood on his land belonging to Nelson who had left. Mr. Nelson worked at the store in Cooperstown. Since I didn't have any money, I took the only thing I had of any value, which was my pipe, and fled to town. I met Mr. Nelson and asked him how much he wanted for the house. He told me twenty-five dollars. I then told him I had no money, but a tobacco pipe that was worth that amount. We made the deal; I got the house and a pair of overalls, and he got the pipe. We were both well satisfied with the deal.

Mr. Johnson had two oxen, and I had my shanty moved to my quarter on section ten. Later on in the fall came the old bachelor that had squatted on the quarter I filed on and sold the shanty to me.

I was working on the railroad until it came as far as Cooperstown. We workers got meals and lodging in a couple of wagons. One day we went with the train south to Dazey to get me work. When night came on, the boss went with the train to Sanborn and left us there on the prairie. That day it was ninety-five degrees heat. During the night it was not far from frost. In my haste I had forgotten my jacket in Cooperstown. I had just a thin cotton shirt on. Three o'clock in the morning the train came from Sanborn, and I was nearly frozen stiff. In the morning I had a fever and could hardly raise my head from the pillow. Sometime in the forenoon I got up and told the Norwegian cook I wanted to try and get home. On my way home I fell over several times and had to lie down a while. I at last came to Aarestads. They had put a floor and windows in their sod house. There I laid a whole month with typhoid fever. It never entered our mind to send for a doctor.

It was a few days before Christmas in the year 1883 that Mr. Aarestad and I were going to town to buy provisions for the holidays. We got a ride with Elling Johnson, who had the largest yoke of oxen I've ever seen. It was towards evening coming from town when we reached Johnson's, where we ate our supper. About eight o'clock we started for home, one mile from there. It was very dark—not a star to be seen. We started out in the right direction but very soon we found we were going the wrong way. We noticed we had gone west instead of south. Then we tried to go the direction of the railroad, but that went a different way. At eleven o'clock we ran against a wall of a claim shanty. We went in but the only thing we found was a hat on the wall. We took up a few pieces of board from the floor and tried to make a fire. We had three matches; we wasted two. The third match lit and saved us from being frozen. It was under zero weather. We had wool overcoats on, but in the shanty were cracks in the walls where the wind blew in. When we were too cold on one side, we turned on the other. The smoke from the fire filled the whole room. When morning came, we had burned up eight twelve-inch boards. It was a cold morning, about thirty or forty degrees below. We had to keep turning around to keep from freezing our faces. At home our wives had also a sleepless night.

It was in 1881 and 1882 that most of the new settlers settled together south and east from Cooperstown. In 1883 the railroad came through. Here they stood, these brave sons and daughters from their respective homelands, thousands of miles away from their country and relatives, far from people, forty miles to the nearest town, Valley City, and almost penniless. They had burned bridges behind and had many questions in mind of what the unknown future would have in store for them in this new country. The future did not look very brightening for them, but with new courage they started to build homes for themselves and their children on the lone prairie, which hereafter would be their working field. There were many obstacles that came in their way, but the bigger the obstacle, the more interesting it was to overcome it. Such circumstances showed who could stand the test. There was a strife between life and death. It would be a long story if the new settlers were to tell of their experiences from those days about their sacrifices, hopes, disappointments, strife, and victories, but there man and wife stood side by side, enduring the hardships together. I have many times thought that the wives of the pioneers should have just as much place in the pages of history as the man.

Among the immigrants represented all types of life's work—tailors, blacksmiths, shoemakers, captains, tanners, etc. They aimed to take possession of the land where the Indians, buffalo, and antelope a thousand years had had their rights. They aimed to seek a better land. The first settlers headed for the Sheyenne River where there was plenty of wood. When I came two years later, I found log cabins along the woods and sod houses out on the prairie.

It was a hard time for all the new settlers. If you were to borrow anything, you had to give security, and the collectors were like blood-suckers. It is terrible how these collectors would rob the settlers of their hard-earned money, and many gave up not being able to take care of the high rent in borrowing. I put in my first crop, and the oxen, not being broke in, had to be led back and forth on my fourteen acres of breaking. In the midst of my work the sheriff came and told me I had to come to town. Someone wanted to see me, and he told me who it was. I untied my oxen and walked five miles to town. The sheriff could have just as well given me a ride in his buggy, but no.

This certain person had bought a note that I had given to Lawrence Bros. that should be paid in the fall. I presume he had bought it for a less amount. Instead of sending me a letter, he sent the sheriff out without warning me. I was green and did not know the law. In the fall when I paid it, the sum was double. This is no false remark, but the straight goods. I do not like to write about this, but it belongs to a new settler's life. Some years later a businessman had a mortgage on my crop. In the fall I needed a little lumber. When I went to town, I took with a few sacks of oats to pay for it. The mortgage man had heard that I was to do this, so without warning he hired the sheriff to hire two horses and to come out and drive in all my wheat crop. I had eight hundred bushels and had sold none. This was too much, the sheriff thought. He came out to the farm and talked to me. I thanked him for his friendliness, and the next day I hauled the wheat in myself.

We moved to our own farm in the year 1884 when the weather was warm enough to live in a shanty. Our two oxen and one cow with a calf, we tied on the prairie within the reach of water. If a man gets up in the wee hours of the morning in the spring when nature wakes up after a winter's sleep and you examine mother nature's plants, animals, bird life, prairie chickens, each one in their own place, and the ducks splashing in the water, it all seems like a prairie romance. Here was also our place. Our life's work was to clean away and built up our new land. We cultivated the wild prairie, following our creator's commandment to till the soil. With my oxen and two borrowed oxen I got my fourteen acres of land broke up. It was the same piece I was working on when the sheriff came. That summer I used a fork and scythe to gather the hay. Elling Johnson and I helped each other on the farm during haying season. One night when I came home, there were two calves on the farm, and my wife, who always was alone when I was away, told me that a man came by, driving in a wagon with a cow tied behind and a calf following. She ran after him and asked him if he wanted to sell a calf. He told her he was alone on his claim and didn't want to bother with the calf and that he was on his way to Cooperstown to sell it. She bought the calf for five dollars. It so happened she didn't have any money. He waited while she ran a half-mile to the neighbor to get five dollars. The cow had milk enough to feed the calves. I thought my wife made a pretty good deal.

It was October 1885. For three days the air was filled with smoke and a strong wind was raging from the northwest. The third day the wind increased, and the smoke became thicker. I was with Swen Olgard out threshing seven miles away. I knew my wife was home alone with a little child. Right after dinner I started for home. I had just stepped in the door and said hello when I was out again, and I fled to the neighbors to borrow oxen to plow around the wheat stacks. But just then I saw flames a half-mile away, and in a few minutes the flames were over us. There was no danger for the house, barn, and haystack. I had summer-fallowed around them and mostly around the side of the house where the storm came from. We were not afraid for our lives, but it was horrid to see flames all around us. We had lot of rain that summer, and the grass stood very high which gave the flames a better chance to spread; but the flames went past like a wind with a thunderous noise. When we came outside, the prairie was black, and worse, the air was full of smoke.

The third stack, somewhat smaller, I had put inside the breaking near the sod barn, so it was spared. This was my first crop. Later a threshing machine came near by, and the neighbors hauled this stack on wagons to the machine and threshed it. I got fifty bushels from it. That's the type of neighbors we had in those days. When one lost a cow, the neighbors would chip together and buy a cow for him.

Many of the settlers' cows that were tied here and there where there was green grass jerked loose and ran. One cow became so badly burned, it had to be butchered. Many lost their crops; some lost them after it was threshed and put in the granary. It was difficult to meet a fire like this. The wind threw large bunches of straw over the breaking. The fire lasted three days with a steady wind. Where it came from, we do not know, but it covered a territory of not less than one hundred miles. The state was unsettled westward. The fire stopped when it reached the Sheyenne River.

In the spring of 1884, when the weather permitted, we moved into the shanty. The roof and walls were of rough boards. Late in the summer I got some men to help me build a sod house. I received information from someone who understood how the sod house should be built. The first thing was to find out the best material to use, and that had to be a certain sod of strong grass roots. We found that along a slough. We had to break the chunks carefully, three or four feet inches thick. We cut it in big chunks. When the chimney was made, sand was put between each layer. We left an opening for a double window in the south and east and for a door on the north where we later built a room with a slant roof and a door on the east. Here in the summer we had the stove. We had five elm logs; we put one on the top, one on each side, and one on the chimney. On these we nailed the rough boards from the shanty and then tarpaper. We had grass three feet long that we laid layer upon layer next to the sod so as to keep out the water. We laid the sod gradually as we cut it; then the house was considered ready so far. It was then to fix the inside, to smooth out the walls as smooth as a plastered wall. We swept the walls good with a broom so that the grass pieces should hold the plastering. We then found some gumbo or white clay on the edge of a large slough, which we used for the walls. This stayed on the walls as long as we lived there (eight years) After, my helper, Mr. Korgsgard,

Threshing in Dakota

suggested we whitewash the walls with the same stuff. It became quite a bit lighter. Later on when we could afford it, we whitewashed it with plaster. It was a good house, warm in the winter and cool in the summer. We never had a fire at night. In those years it never even froze the water in the house. The rain went through just once during a cloudburst.

The year 1891 is a year to be remembered. My neighbor Jens Bull and I hired a machine which was to thresh our shock. We had trouble with the machine more or less all the time. One morning we asked the machine owner to thresh, but he said, "Aw, go home with you." We went home and started to stack the wheat. This was my luck. I think all the old settlers will remember the record year for North Dakota. The wheat bunches were heavy as stone, and the average yield was forty to fifty bushels to the acre. Those that finished their threshing that fall were lucky. They got seventy-five cents per bushel.

It was already the last part of October and no sign of getting anything threshed. There were just a few machines around. The crops were big, and there was lots of rain that fall. Then we heard of two men by the names of Qualey and Johnson near Mardell who wanted to sell their machine. My neighbor, Mr. Ashland, and myself decided to buy their machine for $600. We had to promise to thresh three of their jobs that were left on their route. It went fine. We had good weather and were through in a week. Qualey and Johnson were paid $600. We owned the machine with no debt against it. We moved the machine to our own farm on the other side of Cooperstown, but before we moved the heavy machine, the first snow came. We each had two oxen. It was a job to pull the heavy machine through the loose snow.

Ashland had promised to thresh some stocks for Christian Lee, four miles south of Cooperstown, but I told him he ought to save his own first which stood in shock. "Aw, what's the difference. The collectors will take it all and I'll get nothing." He moved his rig to Lee's place. We sure found out how hard it was to thresh with a damp machine full of snow and frost. It got so cold we had to keep fire in the machine all night. We hauled water from Cooperstown. The water froze in the tank so there was just a little place open for the water. We had to sweep and pound the snow off the stacks. It went real heavy through the machine. The straw carrier began to trouble so we threw it away. We set two men to pitching straw in a fire which we started. This was a hard job, and the men worked hard.

Then we moved it to our farm two miles further west. It continued cold. One night we kept on until eight o'clock to keep light for those working. Most of the men got tired and left, but my neighbors helped me as best they could. To keep the men in good humor, I bought a box of cigars. One of my neighbors who was a "wet" bought some whiskey for himself and the others who used it.

We paid three dollars a day for those short days, but we were glad to do it. I gave up a couple of my oat and millet stacks to help my brother-in-law thresh his wheat stacks. We had threshed about one-half of Aarestads when there came a terrible blizzard. It was so bad the machine was snowed down. Then Aarestad gave up. In a few days the weather cleared. Emil Krogsgard offered to shovel out the machine and drive it over to his stack if we would thresh for him. We threshed about twelve-hundred bushels. We were through in December. Amongst the ones who threshed the next spring was a partner of mine who sold his wheat for feed for twenty-five cents a bushel. This is an example of what we had to go through that fall, and when I stop and think about it, it seems almost unbelievable that we could keep on threshing under those circumstances. Every one helped the best they could. I sold my share in the machine the next spring.

Dakota Was Not For Him

Irving I. Gardner

To say that everybody was land crazy would not be a serious exaggeration.

In 1860 Irving Gardner was born into a family that had farmed near Charlotte, Maine, since before the American Revolution. Because the farm had difficulty supporting the eleven Gardners, Irving at age twenty left home and found employment through his two brothers who had established a grocery store in Meriden, Connecticut. After working around Meriden for a while, he journeyed westwardly: railroad baggageman in New York; flour-mill worker in Chicago; farmhand near Elgin; factory worker in Maywood; teaching school and lumbering near Stillwater, Minnesota. In 1881 he headed for the prairies of Dakota where he was joined later by his brother. Like thousands of others, his stay in Dakota was brief; he homesteaded, paid it off, sold it, and returned to Connecticut, where in 1886 he married and entered the insurance business.

AFTER VISITING AND SCRAPPING IN [lumber] camp was over, I had to start execution of our plans to "go West." This was the plan. I would go up to Hope and see H. P. Smart and arrange for taking a homestead. After "nailing down" my chosen land, provided there was any left, I would avail myself of my legal right to leave the homestead for not more than six months and run out to that wonderful land in Montana. If Montana was all the boom sheet said it was, I would stay there and A. P. [Ansley P., another brother] would join me after finishing up on the log drive at St. Louis. This plan was followed, all but the finishing.

31

A Train in Dakota Winter

So back to Stillwater I went, said goodbye to the relatives and friends there, got my trunk, and started for St. Paul. There I bought a ticket for Glendive, Montana, with stop-over privileges at Everest, where I was to detour to Hope, supposing, of course, that a train ran to or very near Hope. I was to leave my trunk at Everest station until I came back from Hope and pick it up to go along further west. I took my "carpet bag" and bought ticket for the nearest station to Hope. I never knew what that station on the St. Paul, Minneapolis, Manitoba Railroad was. The train was a freight train with a few passenger cars and a caboose in the rear. After traveling about half the distance toward Hope, the passenger cars ran off the rails and bumped along on the ties. We were going pretty slowly and no one seemed much alarmed at first, but some of the men got up on the cars and tried to attract the attention of the engineer by yelling and waving coats. They had no success and things began to look more startling. More cars were off the rails and the cars began to zigzag. The call was to jump off and others did so. I stood on the platform with another, an Irishman from Philadelphia. We both hesitated.

"Jump," I cried.

"No, not yet," he answered.

I made the plunge into a snow bank and went in up to my waist without hurting myself at all. No sooner had I jumped than over went the cars on their sides and were pulled a considerable distance before the train stopped or these cars became unshackled.

The poor Irishman failed to jump and was on the platform when the car turned over. He was crushed by the rail into the snow bank with but a small part of his body in sight when I got up to him. The snow was spattered with blood, and I feared he had been killed, but by pawing the snow away I found that his bruises were all on his feet. Poor fellow moaned and took on agonizingly. I think he must have been in great pain of both body and mind, for he too, like myself, was bound for a "Hope" somewhere.

Everybody stood around looking at him with apparently no thought to give him aid. I think this was my first, and I guess my last, occasion where I assumed responsibility to care for one in distress. Upon my direction we picked the man up bodily and carried him across the track to a small house whose occupants spoke little, if any, English. I found that the man was suffering greatly from the injured feet. I removed his boots and stockings and got the woman of the house to bathe his feet in warm water. Whether or not that was proper treatment, I didn't know, but it seemed right and the woman seemed to think so and helped willingly. I had talked with this man a little on the train, and now he seemed to think I was the only friend he had in that God-forsaken country.

He moaned again and again, "Why did I leave my good home in Philadelphia to come out here to be dumped in a snow bank, with no one to do a thing for me and nowhere to go?"

When I started to go to the train, he begged heart-breakingly for me to stay with him. I had to go as the train was soon to pull out, and so I bade the unfortunate homesick fellow good-bye, never to see him again.

So this was my abrupt introduction into Dakota Territory. But the worst was yet to come. The passenger cars were unshackled from the freight cars and were lying slumbering in snow banks beside the track. Empty freight cars were backed up, and we passengers were bundled in to be carried to our destination. I began now to be inquisitive as to how far ahead was Hope. I then learned that the train didn't go through Hope at all, but that there was stopping place (no station, hotels, or houses) where I could stop and move on to Hope. I also learned that Hope was about eighteen miles from this place and that there was no conveyance there. Since it was almost night, I was told that I could, if I wished, spend the night with the railroad track gang which slept in a freight car. This looked like more adventure to me, and I quickly accepted the accommodations which I think cost me nothing. I didn't altogether enjoy the society of my hosts. I think I must have been a poor conversationalist. I do remember very well my directions to Hope, which were to "follow the sleigh tracks and keep going till you get there. You'll know it when you see it 'cause there are no other houses on the way."

This looked like some venture, indeed, for the sleigh tracks were not at all well marked on account of little travel and blowing snow. I got a good early start and it was well I did. I had read not long before (this was in 1881) of blizzards so severe that men had perished in going from their house to the barn, and I had a terrible fear that one might get after me. I therefore practiced all the kinds of travel gaits I had ever heard of. I walked, trotted, and galloped, and it was well I did for I had not made half the distance when the wind began to blow and those tumble weeds went bounding by like phantoms. Soon it began to sleet and my face was pelted with those fierce, sharp, pointed ice particles which seemed to cut the very skin. I think my instinct must have been pretty keen, as the road marks were almost obliterated, but I went straight to Hope.

At the first house I came to, I inquired, "Where is the Hope House?"

"Up there on the hill."

"Is that it?" I wondered.

I supposed it was a big hotel. I went up and asked for my cousin, Mr. Smart. He came out and greeted me and laughed heartily at my looks and no wonder, for my face was as red as a beet from that hail pelting. In fact, I didn't know myself as I looked in the mirror for I had been fairly bleached out after all winter in school. A hearty greeting and welcome was extended from the earlier arrivals to another sucker.

If the Hope House wasn't a great big hostelry, it did have a land office. It had three or four rooms on the first floor and three on the second floor. Mr. Smart was the landlord and agent for the Hope Land Development Project. S.S. Small, a former Pembroke, Maine, boy and intimate acquaintance of the Smart family, was promoting the project, I suppose, by bringing people there to become settlers, thus enhancing the value of this town properties or perhaps speculating on the land as it would change hands.

To say that everybody was land crazy would not be a serious exaggeration. The cry was, "Get some land and get it quick or you may get left." I thought at that time that all the land within five miles or so had been much taken. I talked seriously with my cousin Smart to get his candid advice. Of course, in his position he could not advise against settling there, and I think he was really sincere in his statement that, "Now is the time to buy." Other men, and I found more there from my state of Maine, all seemed very eager to get into production on a large scale. And why wouldn't they? Wheat was quoted at one dollar per bushel and twenty bushels per acre was reasonable production. You therefore had on a 160 acre tract 3,200 bushels at one dollar or $3,200. Deduct a reasonable charge for seed and other costs and you have a nice little profit on your quarter section. People were so optimistic about the whole plan of wheat raising that they didn't seem to think that the price might not hold at a dollar, that production would not run less than twenty bushels per acre, or that blight or insect might wipe out the whole crop.

A branch line of the Northern Pacific Railroad was being built right into Hope and that would bring hoards of people there, which would build up the town and add to general prosperity. The New Hope House was built that summer and seemed a substantial addition to the town. It was a square, two-story, flat room building with about twenty to thirty rooms.

I decided that I must secure my own 160 acres then or never. Smart scanned his maps and pointed out what he said was the best available, and I signed up for it. I didn't like one thing about it. It had one of those low saucer-shaped depressions near the front, so common there. But I took it and resolved in my mind that I would bore a hole in the bottom of it and let the water out. Folks laughed at me, but I have heard that very thing has since been done. If it hasn't, it ought to be. Smart had agreed to build a house for me, so I said goodbye, as I wanted to study that Montana El Dorado.

The trip back to Hope was far different from the trip going out. The train crossed the Missouri on a bridge instead of a raft. I rode right into Hope on the train, just like a Knights of Labor official. I found a house built on my quarter and moved in and took possession. I had a well dug and contracted for plowing the twenty acres required in the spring.

People were still enthusiastic about the country but there was nothing for most of them to do as they had no stock and, of course, could do nothing on the land in the winter. Perhaps they all did as I did, went South and taught school. After the second winter teaching in Stillwater, Minnesota, I got back early to Hope. I found the town bristling with business, a locomotive steaming and tooting in the freight yard, stores being erected, and a general appearance of progress.

But what was I going to do? I couldn't sit in my shanty and watch twenty acres of oats grow, and if I did, I couldn't make them grow any faster or better. So I "hired out" to A.W. Breed who was starting a big farm between my land and Hope. I worked for him all summer, going out to my land nights, riding Mr. Breed's pony.

Life with the Breeds was pleasant and interesting. Mr. Breed came from Jamaica Plain, Massachusetts, Mrs. Breed from a midwestern city. They were both college graduates. He was tubercular, which was the cause of his being there. The farm was well stocked with horses and every kind of farm machinery then in use. They lived well and apparently enjoyed life, yet I now think that he had not then learned whether his venture was "paying its way" or not. I think he must have been pretty well off, as he always seemed to have plenty of money.

It was just sport for me to hitch up a five-horse team to a sulky plow and strike out to plow a furrow a mile long. (Not much like plowing back home with a one or two-horse team and walking plow on a three- or four-rod stretch.) This prairie land was virgin soil. The sod was tough; many places the ground was full of low wild rose bushes in bloom. It was an easy job because the horses followed the furrow.

While I was there and helped in the harvesting, I had no knowledge as to the result in bushels per acre. Mr. Breed broke away from general practice and planted some potatoes which I think did very well considering the care they didn't get. It would have seemed like poor treatment back home, just to plow under the seed and give no more attention.

I don't know what the people in the village did for amusement. We never went there except on business. Mr. Breed was a fine pianist, and we used to do lots of singing. Mrs. Breed played a great deal also. There was no church in Hope at that time. For a real day of recreation we occasionally took a Sunday "out in the country." We never worked Sundays except to care for the stock. Mrs. Breed prepared a good lunch, and we all piled into the big truck farm wagon and drove off just somewhere, but nowhere in particular. A shady place would have been welcome but there was none except perhaps under a few stunted trees. We ate our lunch, enjoyed the leisure, the sunshine, the bit of shade, and thanked God for the great wide open spaces which we surveyed.

Home life on my quarter section was at first very discouraging and provoking, for I had no sooner moved in when burglars did the same. They were considerate in a way as they didn't take everything at one time. First they took my blankets, then dishes, tools, then the clock. Each time I would try to strengthen my fortress, but the burglars would use a little more force and ingenuity and get inside. I finally got the doors and windows barred up so that they couldn't get in without smashing in, and they apparently stopped just before doing that. But there was still one more way to extract my wealth. They climbed to the roof and pulled up the stovepipe which was connected with my stove. One night I was wet and tired and got home only to find my stove several feet short of pipe to go through the roof. But a young adventurer like me could not let that bother him. I had to do something, for it wouldn't do to let the smoke pour out into the room. So I pulled off a couple of boards from a partition and ran them from my bed to a table, lifted the stove to this higher level, shoved the pipe through the roof again with a piece of wire run through it and under the roof boards for further protection, started my fire and in no time was all heated up ready for business as usual.

One week we were haying somewhere five or six miles outside of Hope. Weather had not been good for a few days, and on Friday morning it looked as though nothing could be done before Sunday. It was, therefore, my job to get back to Hope and walking was the only way to get there. I had not gone very far when I noticed a haystack, and for some reason noticed that something about the surroundings was different from most all of the broad prairie land. I had started in the forenoon, and about noon time I felt somewhat faint as I approached a semblance of a dwelling made of turf. I went to the opening (there was no door) and called to the woman inside and asked for a drink. As she didn't speak English, I had to make motions to make her understand. Finally she went inside to get me the drink. I saw her get a cup and wash out the inside of it with her fingers. I noticed, also, that the livestock occupied special rooms in the apartment. I wouldn't want to swear to it now, but the picture I have in mind is that the cow occupied what would answer to the "spare room" and the pigs "the boys' room." When she came out with a cup of milk, I was like [a friend] at our old Montana camp, not hungry or thirsty, and I did the very discourteous act of giving it back.

Election day was approaching to decide where the county seat should be, Hope or Cooperstown. Of course, we in Hope favored Hope. I had finished my work there and was ready to leave. When I prepared to clear the hotel, the manager said, "You mustn't go before election. Stay and we'll find a job for you at good pay." I, therefore, stayed for three dollars per day and board, until the election was past. The result of the election is a matter of history.

I then went to Fargo to get the deed of my land as I had complied with homestead requirements and was paying cash instead of remaining as a farmer for five years. This land, being within twenty-five miles of the Northern Pacific Railroad, cost two dollars and fifty cents per acre, or $400.00 for the 160 acres. I borrowed this money from A.P., as well as $200.00 more "just to have some pocket money" on my travels. That looked easy, borrowing $600.00, but A.P. seemed to trust me and I am glad to be able to say that I paid him with interest before he had need of it.

My plan was to close up the Fargo business, then start for Connecticut, calling at Stillwater and Chicago en route. In Connecticut I was to get two brothers, Austin and Arthur, fired with the "Out West" spirit, and we would all go back together to grow up with the country. I wanted to surprise them by my coming, so I mailed a letter to go on the same train I did, telling of the wonderful country and what I had been doing, but said not a word about going east.

The ride from Hope down to the Northern Pacific junction was interesting, for the train crew actually did what I had often heard of but did not believe. They stopped the train and got out to shoot prairie chickens. When I awoke next morning down in Wisconsin and looked out the window and actually saw hills and trees, I was thrilled with emotion. I had enjoyed the broad, treeless prairie, but had not realized how much the hills and trees meant to me. From that moment until the present my appreciation of them has continued to increase.

I was much surprised and disappointed to learn from the Meriden brothers that they had altogether given up the idea of throwing up their settled positions, forsaking their friends, and starting out on an uncertain venture with their families.

"You have had a dash at it," they said, "and you had better settle down right here. Perhaps you will do just as well as you would out West."

I was very much opposed to this plan. I thought it was unmanly, cowardly. A fellow with any gump at all in him should get out and keep on seeking for adventure. But I yielded to their persuasions. I was about to write of a few business ventures back here in the sleepy old East, when I thought some inquisitive reader, if perchance there ever is one, might ask, "What did you do with your Hope homestead?" My answer is that I rented the land for cropping and I think I got enough out of it for the carrying charges. About 1889 R. H. Simpson, editor of the *Hope Pioneer*, bought the land for $500, paying for same in installments over two or three years. And that was the end of my Dakota ventures.

To Dakota — Against Her Will

Emelia Griepentrog

♪ cried from dawn to dawn and from dark to dark.

Emelia and Charles Griepentrog lived in Wisconsin where Charlie worked in a factory to support Emelia and the three children, Otto (b. 1878), Herman (b. 1879), Oscar (b. 1881). In 1883 Charlie went west and filed on a homestead in Richland County not far from Hankinson where he labored as a farmhand that same summer. During the winter of 1883-1884 he returned to his old job in Wisconsin and moved his family to Dakota in spring 1884. Like many newcomers, he continued to work as a farmhand while he was establishing himself on his own homestead. Emelia did not want to leave Wisconsin and her adjustment to life in Dakota was painful. Her story was not uncommon.

I DIDN'T WANT TO LEAVE AND COME WEST, but Charlie said he was coming and if I wanted to live with him, I would have to come west. I even went so far as to try to burn the papers he had for his land in Dakota.

I tried every way I could to get Charlie to change his mind. But Charlie's mind was made up, and I had the choice of going with him or giving him up. I decided to go with him. So in April 1884 Charlie loaded the furniture, machinery, lumber, and he bought a cow so that he could get his ticket free by having to ride with the car load of furniture and other things to take care of the cow. Of course Charlie started out before me so that I was alone to take the train and make the trip with the three boys—ages six, four, two.

I made the trip by train and through the whole trip I was near tears, though I didn't give way to tears. I arrived in Dakota a week after Charlie had arrived, but Charlie met me and took me to live with him at the Fred Hoefs farm until he was able to get the house built on his own land. Charlie was hired to work for the Hoefs through the whole summer of 1884. The whole family lived with the Hoefs over four weeks.

Hoefs had had diphtheria during the winter of 1883 and 1884. About the middle of the third week that we were there, our oldest boy was taken sick and they didn't have a doctor but he didn't get any worse. Then about five days after the oldest boy was taken sick, the middle boy was taken sick. The night before, the boy had told me that the new shoes which I had bought him before he came west made him too tired. During the day he had followed Mrs. Hoefs everywhere she went, and, of course, he was tired, and that night he sat in her lap and told me that he was so tired and that his shoes made him tired and he wasn't going to wear them any more. The next morning he didn't come downstairs as usual, so I went up to see what he was doing and found him on the floor by the side of his brother's bed. I called to him and told him not to go near his brother because he was sick. He looked up and said, "I's sick too Mummie, my head hurts, I fall down." By noon that day Herman was too sick to talk. I asked Charlie to go for a doctor, but Fred said they didn't have time for such and that Charlie couldn't leave the fields. Otto, the oldest son, got well but the middle son, Herman, died and was buried just across the fields northeast of our new home. When Otto was well and had been up a week, we moved to our new home. I lived alone for a time in the new home because Charlie had to work at the other farm and could only get home for Sundays.

I cried from dawn to dawn and from dark to dark. I was lonely, afraid to be alone. Of course the death of Herman upset me a great deal, and I had so much time to think of him that it really made it worse for me. I had plenty of food though I couldn't eat. In the mornings as I set feeding the two boys, I could look out of the window and see the grave of my son, and, of course, that was bad. A picture of my dead son was always in front of me.

Charlie came home for a few hours every Sunday to change clothing and see how I was, but he had to go back before dark in order to do the night's work. One Sunday when he was home, I couldn't help but cry because he was up on the roof working and he whistled. I went out and asked him what he had to be so happy about, and then I broke down and cried. That was the first time he had seen me cry or knew that I did cry while he was away.

I cried so hard that day that he was worried about me and decided not to let me stay alone any more, so he went back towards Hoefs' farm, but when he got there he didn't stop but went right on west until he reached Redemskies farm about ten miles from home. There he found an old lady who was staying with the Redemskies and was willing to go with him and take care of me. The lady and Charlie returned about seven that night, and I was so glad to see them though it was a surprise; but this lady lived with us until after the baby was born, and I was able to do my work alone again. After that I wasn't so afraid to be alone because I knew that it would be just a few more weeks and Charlie would be home for good.

We Griepentrogs were well supplied with food for the first winter, and I wrote to my mother and told her not to worry about me, for we wouldn't starve as my cellar was so full that I could reach the food by getting on my knees on the kitchen floor and bending down to the cellar opening. Mr. Hoefs gave us all the potatoes we could use for the winter and enough wheat for flour. Albert Bohm gave us a pig and two weeks after we had gotten this pig, it had a litter of little ones, and all ten of them lived and were ready to butcher that fall so we had plenty of pork for the winter. We had brought a cow with us, so we had a supply of milk for our cooking and cream with which to make our butter. The other food articles which we needed we bought in Wahpeton with the money that Hoefs had given Charlie for his summer's work.

Land And More Land: A Speculator

Thomas Mitchell Hadwen

At one time father owned twenty-seven sections of land.

Thomas Hadwen's father, Robert, was a prosperous Ontario, Canada, farmer who owned over four-hundred acres near Wingum and a drugstore in the town. Thomas (b. 1852) helped his father on the farm, and when he was twenty, managed the drug business. In 1873 he married a local girl, Amelia Miller. In 1876 he joined the landseekers bound for Dakota. After he filed his claim, he convinced his father that Cass County was ripe for farm development and land speculation. Robert Hadwen became one of the Red River Valley's largest land holders. He knew how to get land.

I N THE SPRING OF 1876 I DECIDED TO COME to the Dakota Territory and took a train at Wingum and rode to Kincarden on the shore of Lake Huron, a distance of about twenty-five miles from Wingum. I boarded a boat there and rode to Duluth, Minnesota. The trip took about four and half days on the boat. I then took a train from Duluth and traveled to Fargo [June 15, 1876].

The only building in Fargo at that time was Old Headquarters—sometimes called the Colonist Reception House. It was just a big log building that settlers could come in and cook their own meals on the big stove that sat squarely in the center of this building. This same building was later built into a hotel and called the Headquarters Hotel. They boarded the outside up with clap wood and built additions onto it. It was also made into a depot and freight house. This building burned

43

to the ground in Fargo's great fire.

I filed a preemption costing me two and one-half dollars an acre. I stayed in and around Fargo for about a month, then went back to Wingum, Ontario. The date was about the first of August in the year of 1876. I had no hard trouble coaxing father to come out to the Dakota Territory. Father, being very well-to-do, was always looking for speculations. He saw the great possibilities of making good money in the Dakota Territory.

In the spring of 1877 father came to the Dakota Territory. With him, he brought three carloads of horses, eighteen men, and two women for cooks. He then bought up four or five sections of land in and around Fargo and Casselton. He set these men out to breaking up his land and had them build shanties. That same year he had his men build a shanty on my land. It was a twelve- by eighteen-foot shanty. All these shanties were made out of rough lumber.

I stayed in Canada and put the crop in on my father's land there that spring, while father came to the Dakota Territory. That spring father wrote back and told me when I had the crop in to go out and buy another carload of horses, for horses were in great demand at that time. I brought along my wife and two children and the carload of horses.

The following spring, in 1878, I, father and mother, brother Robert Fleetwood, two sisters Anna and May Jeaneth, and my wife and two children came to the Dakota Territory with a couple carloads of machinery and furniture.

This same year father had bought a lot more land. At the end of the year of 1878 father bought and owned about eighteen sections of land in and around Fargo. Father had bought a lot of "Indian Script" from the half-breeds. Some of this script he bought for a jug of whiskey; other he had to pay a little money for it. But on the whole whatever he paid for it, it was for a great bargain.

The year of 1878 was the first year I reaped any harvest in the Dakota Territory. The crops that year were very good. Average yield an acre was about thirty to thirty-five bushels.

I was told that a few years before I came to Dakota Territory there were about eighteen thousand head of buffalo killed in the [Red River] Valley. It was possible, for the prairie was covered with buffalo bones.

The bones had to be cleared off the land in some places just like rock. In about the year of 1900 they found a use for bone and so the pioneers made some money off of the bone they had stacked around. There were many hundred carloads of buffalo bones shipped out of the Dakota Territory. Every town along the line had huge stacks of bones along the railway tracks ready to be loaded and shipped.

In the spring of 1878 when my family was making the trip to the Dakota Territory, we were between Detroit Lakes and Fargo when the train took to a sudden halt. Everybody was anxious to know the reason. To our amazement the conductor of the train said it was on account of the grasshoppers. Everybody laughed to think that a few grasshoppers could stop a train, but they soon found out it was no joke for they were delayed a half of a day. The grasshoppers would sit on the rails, causing the engine to slip on the rails. Where the grade was level, the engine would move all right, but where the grade was a little up-grade, the engine could not make it.

I made a deal with father in 1879 and traded my farm off onto some machinery and cattle. I then started to help father manage the many farms that he had acquired in Cass County. At one time father owned twenty-seven sections of land.

Father had a farm near where now stands the Cass County Court House, which we called the home place for we lived there most of the time. We were threshing about a mile north of the home when a cyclone came up and totally demolished the home. This happened in the year of 1879. Mother and sisters who were home at the time of the cyclone were unhurt. This cyclone tore down big machinery barns in Fargo and strewed farm machinery all along Front Street. This cyclone cost hundreds of dollars of damage.

Narcisse and Sophranio and Their Twenty-one Children

The Hebert Family

The students were always moving their beds according to the direction of the wind.

Narcisse and Sophranio Lacosta Hebert and their twenty-one children arrived in Pembina County in 1877. The Heberts were natives of Grandby, Quebec, Canada, and had first migrated to the United States in 1867 when word went out to French-Canadians that employment could be found in the factories of Woonsocket, Massachusetts. The Heberts worked in the factory cities along the Blackstone River for ten years. Narcisse was an expert wool sorter and son Frank trained himself as a surveyor. In 1877 the Heberts joined an immigrant-colony group that was headed for Manitoba. Frank Hebert tells the family's story about homesteading near Cavalier and his own story about what it was like to be a member of the University of North Dakota's first class.

O N APRIL 23, 1877, A COMPANY OF FIVE HUNDRED people left Massachusetts and went to Manitoba. They were encouraged to go there by a Catholic priest that had been there and had seen the country. He told them that it was the finest land and the best opportunity for large families because all the children that were of age could take up land and in that way get land for themselves. So this company of people hired a train of eleven cars on the New York Central Railroad. When they landed in Manitoba, they were put in a government immigration building where they could stay until they found land that suited them. Father went to northwestern Manitoba and to Winnipeg, and he went to Pembina. After reaching Pembina, he decided to go south of Pembina to see the lay of the land in that part of the country. Father wanted timber land so he would have the logs to build his house and barn. As soon as he returned, we packed up and left for Pembina to make our new home in Dakota. The first place we reached was Fort Pembina and there decided to stay until we found just the right place. Bill Moorehead ("High Water" Bill as he was called) rented us an old house for four dollars per month. This house was very dirty as it had been used for a hen house the year before. There were twenty-five bushels of frozen potatoes in the cellar that had to be removed before we could move into the house. This was all cleaned up, and here the family lived for three months. Father and the three eldest sons all filed on land near Cavalier, North Dakota. They built a log house on father's place, and the first part of August we moved to our new home.

The old pioneer house was made of logs, plastered with clay and white washed. We borrowed an ax to cut all the logs, but a Mr. Douglas did most of the building as we had never built a log house before. The house was twenty-four- by twenty-four-feet square with two rooms downstairs and two rooms upstairs. Each room upstairs had a curtain through the middle, thus making four rooms upstairs in all. It was shingled with homemade oak shingles. These shingles were made with a machine that John Bechtel owned. This John Bechtel, one of the earliest pioneers, had a small sawmill and also a flour mill; so he was a great help to the folk who came into the country to settle here and make their permanent home. There were two windows upstairs and three windows downstairs. In the kitchen window there was one pane that was fixed on swinging hinges because we had "Tommy" the cat trained to go in and out as he wished. There were two doors in the house. All the floors were made from basswood trees. The family lived in this house until 1891 when the family moved to the town of Cavalier.

The furniture was scant and inexpensive. It consisted of a small four-legged cook stove, a homemade table put together with wooden pegs (no nails were used). Beds were very simple: two hard wood poles about five feet in length were stuck into holes made in the wall about six feet apart; the ends of these long poles were cut and the pieces served as legs for the bed. Boards were then laid lengthwise on these poles which served as the bottom of the bed; these were fastened with wooden pegs to hold them in place. Ticks of straw and then of feathers were laid on this to make the bed as comfortable as possible. We had one dresser with a lot of drawer space which we brought from the east. The cooking dishes were all iron; we had some earthenware and white dishes for table use, wood mixing spoons, and meat forks; all the table knives and forks had wood and bone handles. In the east we used candles, so we brought their molds and tallow and what candles we had on hand. When they were all used, we bought small kerosene lamps. It was the women's work to make the candles. The fuel wood was cut from the farm, using the stumps for the box-stove heater. Mostly poplar wood was burned, although some oak and ash was also used. We had to cut the trees so they had some land to cultivate and raise some crop.

When the family landed in Manitoba, it had only $500 left; so after staying there a while and father going into western Canada, we had not so very much left. When we reached Pembina, we bought a pair of oxen with a wood yoke for $104.00 and a cow and calf for $15.00. We got this cow and her calf cheap because the man that owned them was waiting for his right to pass from Minnesota to Canada, and he was at Pembina. One of his cows became fresh, and it was impossible to take the cow because the calf could not follow. So he had to sell them for whatever he could get. So by fall we were very short of money and low on food, especially tea. Mother could not live without it, so I took six straw hats that my mother and older sisters made from braided flax straw and hay and walked to Fort Pembina which is a distance of about thirty miles. About every mile a stake was driven into the ground, and a piece of black sod was placed on the stake. It was also marked by a row of turned up sod on each side of the trail. I left home very early before the sun at about four o'clock. After reaching Pembina, I tried so hard to sell the hats but could not and was very disappointed for I knew that my mother was waiting for my return with the tea. So the man that operated the flat boats on the Red River took them and gave me tea and tobacco with the understanding that when I had the money, I should come and pay, and then I would have to take the hats back. This man felt sorry when I told him how far I walked in order to get tea for my mother and tobacco for my father.

Our first crop was in 1878 and was a load of potatoes of about sixty bushels. We sold these potatoes to the steamboat company at Fort Pembina for a dollar fifty per bushel and in return bought food for the winter. The next year in 1879 we raised some wheat and feed grains that was threshed with a flail. One man could thresh about ten bushels in a day. Most all the food was raised on the farm. Wheat was taken to the mill and given in exchange for flour. Wild fruits were picked in the woods and canned and made into jelly. We butchered our own meat, both pork and beef. Families of ten or twelve would butcher eight to ten porks and one and two beeves. This amount of meat would last a year. The hams, shoulders and side meat, were salted and smoked. Some was fried and packed into stone jars and hot lard poured over the meat to keep it from spoiling. Sausage was kept in the same manner. Flour was five dollars per hundred pounds and tea was one dollar per pound. All the sugar we had in those early days was made from the maple trees in the east, and here in the Dakotas they made a syrup which they drained from the box elder trees. This sap was boiled down until it was thick. This box elder syrup was used for the sweetening part of our foods.

In the fall of 1883 I went to the University of North Dakota at Grand Forks. It was the opening of the first term of school. I went to school for two years, taking all subjects in regard to mathematics which would be of any help to me when surveying land. There were forty-two students enrolled that first term of school.

There was only one building the first two years: the basement served as the kitchen and dining room, the first floor as the classrooms, and the second floor as the sleeping quarters. This second floor was very cold, and the students were always moving their beds according to the direction of the wind as the wind blew through the building with great speed.

The University of North Dakota's First Building

The trees from the city to the University were planted in 1884, and I helped plant these trees while going to school. I had only $200 which paid board and room for nine months at fifteen per month; the rest of my money I needed for books and tuition. I especially remember Cora Smith: she was an English teacher and only fifteen years old. Her mother and father were well educated people. She taught a very long time in the University and then married a man by the name of King. They went east and later made their home in Washington, D.C. She is one of the great leaders in woman's suffrage. She goes by the name of Cora Smith King in the papers. Professor Macnie was the algebra teacher. He used his own textbook. He knew nothing about farming and asked me what the man was doing and asked why he did that. The man was plowing near Grand Forks.

For Health and Hearth

The Herring Family

♪ see again in my mind's eye that great circle of barren, trackless prairie, bounded only by the horizon line.

John Robinson Herring's ancestors came to America "with the first of the Pilgrims." Born in 1818 at Parsonsfield, Maine, he was reared as a Quaker and attended Friends' School at Providence, Rhode Island. When he was twenty, his parents homesteaded near Rockford, Illinois, and John taught school, surveyed, and farmed. He became director of the school and in 1853 married one of its teachers, Nancy Grippen. Nancy was born into an Old Stock American family in 1830 at Annsville, New York. She was a member of the first class that enrolled in Sill Seminary at Rockford, Illinois. In 1882 John Herring, at age sixty-four, decided to forsake Illinois for Dakota to regain his health and to claim one hundred sixty acres of land. Mary Herring Hudson, then a teenager with two older brothers, recounts the story of the Herrings in Dakota.

A S I LOOK BACK NOW TO THE DAYS when there was no North Dakota or no Sargent County, I see again in my mind's eye that great circle of barren, trackless prairie, bounded only by the horizon line, as I saw it first when I went to live with father on his squatter's claim in the summer of 1882.

Father was never a success as a farmer, and when he turned the farm over to a brother, we moved to Oregon, Ogle County, Illinois, and he started a set of abstract books. The hard work and close confinement told on his health very severely, and it was decided he must get out of doors for a while. Just at that time it was found that good flour could be made from spring wheat, and that spring wheat could be grown in Dakota Territory, so with the enactment of the Six Month Preemption Law, father and mother decided to spend their summer in Dakota and gain health and one hundred and sixty acres of land by one and the same motion.

In studying the map of Dakota father noticed that Ransom County was very large and that the county seat, Lisbon, was to the north of the center. He decided that some time it would be apt to be cut in two and he would strike for a claim in the center of the south half. This he planned before leaving Illinois; you will see how it worked out.

Mother had a cousin, J. H. Miller, living at Wahpeton who was clerk of the court and also representative in the state legislature which then met at Yankton, and he wrote saying mother could be his deputy while father located his claim, so father locked up his abstract books, and in March 1882, we started west. From Minneapolis on, it was a long, tiresome journey as we traveled second class on a mixed train [freight and passenger] and had to carry our food with us. We were thrown in with emigrants direct from steerage passage who were so dirty and unkempt and who carried—besides much luggage—such a burden of odors that it was almost suffocating. But father and mother explained it was not their fault and that they deserved our sympathy and help which was always their attitude to our foreign neighbors later.

The train stopped at Breckenridge, and mother's cousin was there to meet us with a buck-board and team of mules to take us across the Red River to Wahpeton, the end of the railroad. It had been thawing and the frost was out of the ground to such a depth that it seemed that nothing but the buck-board body would keep us from sinking out of sight, and we understood why the mules were needed. Empty wagons were often stuck on Main Street at that time.

It was not until May that it was considered safe for father to start out to locate a claim. He got a chance then to go with a Mr. Moore and his two sons, Will and Gene, and a Mr. Barnstable who were going to locate claims. Mr. Moore had lived west of Wahpeton on the Wild Rice River several years and knew the country. In some way they fell in with

Harvey Lord who was a "locator" at ten dollars per claim. Father, with his knowledge of surveying, kept his bearings and insisted on going to the center of the lower half of Ransom County, and they did, passing Ransom City, which was partly-built. They found settlers at "Dunbar," stayed over night there, then turned south and passed over where Forman now stands; but it was so stony father said he would not sacrifice a good farm for the sake of being near a county seat, so after camping near there overnight, they went back to Ransom, and he "squatted" on the land one mile east of Ransom City.

While the others went back to Wahpeton (fifty-four miles) for lumber and material to build their claim shanties, father stayed for a while at Mr. Holding's store. To busy himself he asked if he might use bits of boards and "two by four" that were being thrown away to make a table for his shanty when he should have one. He was given permission and so went to work, making a "cross-legged" table with a trough underneath where the legs crossed—saw-horse fashion. He also went each day over the four claims that the party had staked and dug a little on the four wells so as to show that they had been taken and were being improved.

As you know it can be very cold in May in Dakota, and it was that May. The board bunk which the workmen had been so kind as to share with him was hard and there was not much under or over him so he did not sleep well. One night that was particularly trying, he dreamed that Ransom County had been divided and that the new county was being organized around his table. He did not think the dream at all strange as it was so in line with what he had been thinking. Finally his lumber and tools came, and he began to build his own house—for it was to be a house (sixteen by sixteen feet) with an attic and a shed, with three windows and a floor. In the meantime he lived in Will Moore's shanty (one of the boys) and thereby helped to hold down that claim and his own.

Mother thought that it would not do for father in his condition to live there alone, so it was decided I should go and stay with him while she earned the money in her cousin's office to meet expenses. My older brother had come from Illinois and wanted to get a claim, so mother's cousin, Mr. Miller, decided to take us out. We started early one morning with the mules and a "Democrat" wagon. As we were going to Main Street in Wahpeton, to my horror he stopped in front of a saloon—it was a great shock to my Puritan pride to be sitting out in front of a saloon waiting for someone to come out, but what was even worse he brought out a case of beer and put it in a wagon! I was thirteen and had never seen anything like that before. However, I saw many things new and strange to me thereafter—the vastness of the prairie, its bareness and fenceless road, miles upon mile we went! About noon we stopped at Murphy's on the Wild Rice River, the half-way house. They seemed delighted to see Mr. Miller and gave us the best they had to eat and drank, which made me realize that, although he drank beer and swore quite often, he was very much respected wherever he went.

After that there was more prairie and less road. The day got hotter and hotter as we rode toward the blazing sun. Thee was nothing to drink but slough water, but my cousin and big brother seemed to enjoy the beer. They offered it to me, but I disdainfully refused. At last I thought I could not stand it any longer and took the bottle and raised it to my lips—the smell was enough—I sadly handed it back. It must have been June and the days were long and the ride had been so long—so long! We had stopped at a crossing of the Wild Rice again—at Mr. Post's later called Hamlin—and then on again. At last we drove into the Wild Rice the third time, it must have been near the Will Harring place, and the mud and water were so deep it frightened me terribly—but the mules after much floundering got us through all right. I had been used to pebbly creeks and this seemed to have no bottom at all, just mud and bull rushes. On again—but soon we came in sight of a building, the first we had seen since leaving Mr. Post's (we had seen but three or four houses all day) and cousin told us it was Ransom City. We drove right up to the door which was open—there was no platform. The men got out, and my cousin in helping me out swung me into the open door, which was even with the wagon, into the midst of a lot of Indians, the first I had ever seen. Some thrill to add to all the others of that day!

The men at the store showed us where to find father's claim, and we soon started out again as it was getting late and there was just a faint trace of crumpled grass by which we could find the way to the shanty (Will Moore's) where he was staying. After we got over the hill, it looked like a fly-speck on the landscape. It proved to be eight by ten feet in size with two chicken-coop windows (four small panes), and inside there were two bunks, one above the other like a cupboard, and an old cook stove, a shelf along the wall for a table, a soap box nailed to the wall above for the cupboard, one board on the ground between the stove and bunks, another at the foot of the bunks by the shelf-table. There was hay in the bunks, and after my fifty-four mile ride I was too tired to care to eat, so father told me to crawl into the upper bunk with my clothes on and he would cover me up. I was soon dead to the world and my heart ached—for it was the end of the world for me: no school, no chums, nothing I had ever known before except for father.

For food we had a choice of old bread or crackers, summer sausage that had been stored in a tarpapered room until it could have served as moth balls as well as food, great chunks of fat salt pork—so fat a slice would be six inches through—and that was all. There were no vegetables because they were too expensive to buy canned except on rare occasions. Dried apples, blackberries, and prunes were the luxuries. I used to soak crackers in vinegar for pickles sometimes.

My cousin, before starting back to Wahpeton that morning, showed me how to mix flour and water and a little salt for pancakes as they did in the Civil War (he was a veteran of that war), and then told me to set it out on the roof of the shanty in the sunshine to sour. When it began to "bubble" I was to put soda into it and I would have fine "flap-jacks" he said. He also showed me how to toss them up to turn them. It became one of my chief diversions; trying to "flap 'em" and get them to land in the pan again, other side up. It took time and much sour-dough, but I got to be quite a "flapper" after a while.

When my brother and cousin left to go back to Wahpeton, I felt as the Indian looks in the picture, "The End of the Trail." I watched them disappear as a tiny speck over the horizon line and then went into the shanty and wept until there were no more tears to come. They had taken father along to his work, and I was to take his lunch to him when the sun was "near noon." We were only seven miles from the Indian reservation; and there had been a rumor of trouble there, so Cousin Henry had left me two old revolvers—one a long-barreled and another that looked like Captain Kidd's— and told me to practice shooting. The first thing I noticed when I dried my tears was those revolvers, and they awed me into forgetfulness. The terror of handling them became fascinating. I *would* try—and *did*—to shoot! Then when I took father's dinner, I tore a strip off my apron and tied them to my waist for that was a real adventure—the grass was so tall—when I had to cross Grass Creek it was over my head—no telling what was hiding there! You may think it did not take courage—but there were the revolvers! Such a mighty defense they seemed! So I carried them for weeks and learned to shoot quite well.

It was two weeks before Mrs. Holding and her hired girl came to live above the store. During that time the nearest woman was at Lake Tewaukon (Skunk Lake), seven miles to the south near the Indian reservation—a Mrs. W. D. Sprague. But with Mrs. Holding came great joy to every one of the settlers. She was so kind and thoughtful, so cheerful and unselfish, everyone loved her; and during all the thirty-seven years I lived there, she was the leading light in all of Ransom's varying fortunes. If she is ever requited for all the deeds of kindness, it ought to keep her in happiness through all eternity.

Just a mile south of "The Store" were four New York state boys who had come in March and were holding down four claims with one motion as it were. They had joined two claim shanties together across the section line running east for their house, and two others were joined together across the section line running west for their bar, and they lived as one family. They had oxen and had done breaking, had a garden, and sodded up their buildings and were considered very "well-to-do" even at that early date.

I could not bake bread, I thought, in our little hay-burner—a two by four foot sheet-iron stove—after we moved on to our own land, so father made arrangements for me to go over to the New York boys to buy it. I was terribly shy and feared it would embarrass the man who did the cooking to have me see him doing it. I had never known a man to do such a thing before, so I never went inside; but they were very nice to me and once asked father and me to come over the next Sunday and eat dinner with them. They would have green peas—think of it—not a green vegetable since we left Wahpeton! It was one of the big events in my life, but when I got home we couldn't tell which day it was and how were we to know when Sunday came? Father studied over it sometime and finally said, "I think it is tomorrow, so you can go over there for bread and if you find out it is Sunday, you can stay—I'll go to the store and if it is Sunday I'll go down there—if not I'll come home and they will not know that we didn't know the day." I went—it *was* Sunday—father came, and we had a wonderful dinner; we ate outside on the shady side of the house, on a board covered with newspapers, I believe. The one thing I remember was the blue bowl full of green peas—the best, and I believe the first ever grown in Kingston—or if across the line in Ransom township. Think of it, the first ever grown on that soil!

That summer the surveyors came and finished; there had only been two preliminary lines run through the county before that, I believe. Father went with them over all the adjoining lines and seemed to enjoy it very much. By that time he was thoroughly interested in Dakota, for his health had improved very much, and he saw great possibilities for the future there.

One day I got lost coming home from the "New York Boys" with my bread—a terrible sensation I can tell you—not a house or living thing in sight. Father had told me if I ever got lost to go to a top of a hill and watch for smoke, and he would keep a big fire if I ever failed to come back. He was always so thoughtful and kind to me. I went to the top of a hill—but I didn't have to wait for smoke. I could see our house from there and got home all right. After that father would not let me go for bread any more, and we decided to try to bake our own—something I had never tried before. I set my yeast in the morning, going by directions on the package. It was cold, and I had to put it in on the bed to keep it warm. Well, to make a very long and trying story short, I sat up all night to bake it as I could only bake one small loaf at a time, had but one tin, and had to build the fire fresh each time because we burned twisted hay with a very few chips from the building lumber and it went out at once. Lumber was too expensive to use as it cost ten dollars per load just to haul it from Wahpeton. To add to my discomfort, father snored terribly, making great gashes in that primeval silence round about and sometimes I heard the coyotes barking in the distance. Our only book, *The Life of Abraham Lincoln*, proved a fitting companion for the occasion and he seemed very near and real to me that night.

After school was out in Wahpeton my younger brother came and spent the vacation with us, and we all went back to Wahpeton for the winter. Father went back to Illinois. He and my brother shipped some goods and equipment to Andover the next spring, driving the sixty miles from there to Ransom City. The Wahpeton Railroad, a branch of the Northern Pacific, had pushed on to our county, and mother and I went out to the end of the road and hired a team to take us across to Ransom. The fall before (November 1882) mother had been elected Superintendent of Schools of Ransom County to succeed a Mr. Bascom. On January 1, 1883, she went to Lisbon to assume her duties. She also met Mr. Holding there and later boarded with them during the winter. On January 10 mother met father in Fargo, and they made final proof on their preemption and filed on the homestead, upon which they lived the requisite seven years and always thereafter. Father went then to Illinois and mother back to Lisbon where she also worked in the office of Clerk of the Court and my younger brother Eygji and I remained with the cousins in Wahpeton to attend school. We returned to Ransom in the spring.

Early in 1883 the Territorial Legislature had divided Ransom County and called the lower half Sargent, [after a] Superintendent of the Northern Pacific Railroad in acknowledgment of his interest in the development of the Red River Valley. Then in July came the appointment of the county commissioners as before mentioned, but it was not until October 8 that they finally met at the new schoolhouse in Ransom City. Father went to the meeting and said later he thought it strange that his dream had so nearly come true. As you note, the meeting was in October and that means cold weather in Dakota. There was no stove and no other place to go but the store, so father invited them to our house—it had been moved from father's preemption to the adjoining quarter on the north (the relinquishment of which he had purchased from a Mr. Moore and had taken as his homestead) to the place where it still stands—one mile east of Ransom on the north side of the railroad track.

It was not finished—father had done the work alone, except for my help. There were two windows to the south, one to the west and the opening for the door was to the northwest. There was the addition of a lean-to on the east side, and the stairs were merely open steps on the north side of the sixteen- by sixteen-foot room. When we saw a number of teams coming from Ransom, we hurried to get our "front room" in order—for it looked as though we were going to have company. Father came in first and said: "My dream has come true—the commissioners are going to meet here to organize the county around my cross-legged table." So they sat around that table before the two south windows; the doorway and stairs were crowded with people, for there were delegations from Milnor, Kandiotta, Forman and Ransom. Each town wanted the county seat.

Because of his previous experience, father was able to help the new officers start their books, and the first money I ever earned I made writing the first poll-books by hand because father thought the printer at Milnor asked too much for doing it. He had told them he would get it done for half. It was a pretty tiresome job, but I was very proud to be earning anything.

As mother had been elected Superintendent of Schools of Ransom County and could not hold the position and live in Sargent County, they appointed her to that position in the new county. I went with her sometimes, visiting and starting new schools. Often she rode the seventeen miles to Milnor on horse-back. She taught school and rode horseback to school in Hall District until she was seventy-two years old.

Father's last work for the county was his map published in 1898—a fitting memorial to both father and mother which speaks of their ability and conscientious work in the county. Father passed on at his home there on November 30, 1902. Mother soon followed him on December 14, 1903, at the St. Luke's Hospital in Aberdeen.

From Farming to Business: A Roumanian Jewish Family

Hartz "Harry" Naftel Katz

I did not like the farm work or life.

In 1881 when Hartz Katz was thirteen, several Jewish families left Roumania for new homes in the American West. Cyrus and Katy Katz bought a homestead claim near Washburn. For seven years the Katzes tried to make the farm go, but in 1889 he sold out and went into business in Duluth and later Brainerd. Their son Hartz disliked life on the farm and worked at odd jobs in Bismarck where he pursued a business career that eventually led to a successful drug company business with his son Jay in Valley City.

THE FAMILY JOINED FORMER NEIGHBORS who lived near St. Peter, Minnesota. Leaving mother and smaller children with their countrymen, father and I (generally called "Harry") made a trip to Dakota—which had been our goal when leaving Europe. We worked through harvest upon the Kindred farm at Valley City. Father became acquainted with Kindred that summer, and the chance meeting later became a very fortunate one. After harvest father went as far west as Bismarck and bought a homestead relinquishment covering a quarter section near the present site of Washburn. We returned to St. Peter after work "closed up" and wintered at St. Peter. The spring

Settlers bring buffalo bones to the railroad for shipment. The bones brought about nine dollars a ton.

of 1882 father bought a team of horses and loaded what household goods we had gathered into a wagon and drove to the homestead—north from Bismarck. We constructed a house of sod walls and lumber roof, a shed to shelter the horses and a yoke of oxen which had been bought. Father began breaking sod. I did not like the farm life or work and soon returned to Bismarck and worked at such "general labor" as was offered. I was but fourteen years of age, and not large, so I had to take "kid's jobs." I carried water—drinking water—to the workmen upon the old state capitol building; then I received $1.25 per day and was paying twenty dollars a month for room and meals at a rooming house. Later I got a job as yard man at the Sheridan House and a cook—Joe Katz, no kin—took an interest in me and soon had me working in the kitchen. This job lasted until winter when I returned to the farm and helped get wood from a ravine into the Missouri River about three miles from the farm home. A farmer living upon land adjoining father's claim had blasted away the side of a bluff and exposed a vein of lignite coal, and the neighbors for some distance around were allowed to haul as much coal away as they desired. This made the fuel and heat problem an easy one.

In 1883 father had eighty acres of wheat planted and harvested thirty bushels per acre; and the farm seemed a real "find" to the family—though I still did not like farming. So after seeding, I returned to Bismarck and soon had a job with Captain [I. P.] Baker. I worked upon a steamboat which made trips to Fort Benton, Montana. These trips could be made only when the water was high, and in 1885 the boat ran aground upon an island—or sandbar—near Fort Buford. The crew were forced to unload the cargo upon the sandbar and return to

Bismarck to repair the boat; the river "went down" while the boat was making the trip for repairs, and I, who had been left with the cargo, was forced to remain upon the island about six weeks. There was a large number of cases of canned fruit and barrels of crackers in the cargo. The Indians who roamed along the river used [to] row out and trade meat or fish for the other supplies which were part of the cargo. I had a very easy time as the captain had told me he would receive wages until the load was taken away, and when the boat finally got back to load the cargo, I learned that I had been using cases of gunpowder, which was in the load (consigned to the army post at Fort Benton) as a background for the fire which I used to cook coffee or other food. I made trips to Fort Benton during 1884 and 1885, and most of the sixteen-hundred miles along the river we needed to watch almost every rod of the trip because the channel shifted and sandbars "grew" where there had been plenty water a few weeks before.

I "worked" at what jobs were to be had and returned to the farm to help harvest and thresh during the fall until 1888. The years just prior to 1888 were poor crop years, and one fall the family took the team and wagon and roamed the country gathering buffalo bones, which could be traded for groceries in town. We received ten dollars per ton for them. In 1888 father decided to quit farming. He sold off his equipment and took his family to Duluth, Minnesota. In 1889 he opened a small store and junk shop at Brainerd, Minnesota.

I worked with father in the store and gathered junk until 1893 when I with my brother Charles bought a small hardware store at Fargo and operated this store until 1897. Then brother wished to go to Klondike (the "rush" there was at its height then), and we liquidated the store. Charles went to Alaska with his share of the proceeds of the store. After selling the store, I went to St. Paul and spent two years there. I met and married Rosa Pollinger, the daughter of a countryman of mine. We went to Brainerd and spent one year there; then came to Moorhead, Minnesota, where I entered a partnership with John Lalley in the operation of the Golden West Hotel, which we ran for two years, but Lalley handled the money, and it all vanished during the two years.

Preempting, Homesteading, and Tree Claiming

Ernest Kohlmeier

*By the spring of 1887
our ambition had been realized.*

In 1866 William Kohlmeier left his job at Krupps' foundry in
Rocke, Germany, and migrated to America because he had been ordered
to report for military service. By 1881 he had taken land near St. Thomas.
Two years later his younger brother Ernest (b. 1861), no doubt influenced
by Williams' reports about Dakota, left Germany and chose Rolette
County. In 1883 he married Sophie Grimme, his sweetheart from Rocke.
Kohlmeier took advantage of three land laws (preemption, homestead,
timber-culture), not an uncommon Dakota experience.

WHEN I WAS TWENTY-TWO YEARS OLD, I decided to
go out and see the world. A friend of mine was going to
India and asked me to go along. I had just about decided to go there,
but when I mentioned to my employer, a nobleman that I wished to
leave and that I was going to India, he said: "Don't go to India. Go to
a place where they have vegetation. If you are bound to go, go to the
United States. There they have the Monroe Doctrine. In case of war
you are safer there. They do not mix in with our wars. If you go to India,
you might have to fight against us in case of war." So the upshot of it
was that I came to the United States.

As a parting gift the nobleman presented me with a double-barreled, pin fire, breach-loading gun with one barrel bored for shot and one for bullets. The gun was made by hand by C. B. Tanner and Son of Hannover, Germany. The nobleman wanted to give me a pistol also, but I did not accept that, as, I said, "I did not want to be hoggish."

In June 1883 I left Germany from Bremen and came directly to New York on the steamship *Fulda*. It took six days to cross the Atlantic. From New York I came to St. Thomas, Dakota Territory, where I arrived June 16 of that year. With me came my fiancée, Sophie Grimme. The reason we came to St. Thomas was that my brother William was then located there. I worked around St. Thomas until in the fall of 1884.

In September of that year I made my first trip to Rolette County. In the party were five other Germans. We drove a team of mules and a covered wagon. One night on the way up we camped on the shore of Rock Lake in Towner County. We pitched our tent and prepared for the night. We expected to have good beds there, because the reeds were six feet high and there was an abundance of old grass on the ground. For some reason or another we did not go to sleep after we had turned in. We started to tell stories and kept that up until quite late. About eleven o'clock we heard a roar as of a terrible wind. We jumped up and ran outside. Then we saw a big prairie fire racing towards us. We hastily pulled up our tent, loaded it on the wagon, hitched up the mules, and drove into the lake as far and as fast as we could. No sooner had we gotten into the water than the fire swept by us. If we had gone to sleep, we would all have been burned to death.

After we reached Dunseith, we stayed in our tent in Gilbert's grove on Willow Creek at that place. While we were there, I picked out a preemption and tree claim and slept one night on the former. That gave me a squatter's right to it. One evening while we were there, one of the party brought out a .45 muzzle-loading revolver and tried to get the cap off one of the cylinders. Suddenly the gun went off; the bullet struck me in the right forearm and shattered a bone. The only doctor they could find was Dr. Howard who had a claim some distance southwest of Dunseith. I was taken there for treatment. The bullet had gone in on the upper side of the arm and, after shattering the bone, had lodged close to the skin on the underside of it. Dr. Howard looked at the wound and said that it was rather serious. I insisted that the bullet, the lump of which could be felt, be cut out. Dr. Howard brought out a big butcher knife and started to sharpen it. I asked him if that was the only sharp thing he had in the house. I ordered two of the men to take hold of my arm—one above and one below the wound—and hold it securely down on the table, as I was afraid that I would twitch and jerk it if it was not held down. No anesthetic was used. The doctor began to slash—one, two, three, several times lengthwise of the arm. I said, "Cut crosswise. Cut crosswise." The doctor made several slashes crosswise and finally took the bullet out. Hair from my coat and shreds of clothing had been driven into the wound when the bullet went through the clothing and entered the flesh. Dr. Howard said that he had no instrument with which to clean out the wound but said, "We can try to clean it out by poulticing it." I hung around there a week while the wound was being treated. During that time I slept most of the time; I just woke up now and then and went right back to sleep. I thought that Dr. Howard must have put some kind of dope in the food to make me sleep. The wound healed slowly and bothered me for a long time. About a year after the accident happened, three small splinters of the shattered bone stuck out through the skin. I requested a friend to pull them out, but the request was refused. Then I took hold of each of them myself and pulled them out.

After this accident we all lost spirit and returned to St. Thomas. I took the stage from Dunseith to Devils Lake and the train from there through Grand Forks to St. Thomas.

The piece of land that I had selected as preemption was the north half of the north half of section three in what later became Kohlmeier Township in Rolette County. My proposed tree claim was the southwest quarter of the same section. In February 1885 I went by train to Devils Lake and filed on my tree claim. In April of the same year I again went to Devils Lake and filed on the preemption. At the land office I expressed some concern as to whether or not my claim had been taken but was assured that no one had as yet filed on land in that township, and that if it should turn out that somebody had gotten in my way, my filing would be returned to me and I could take another claim. From Devils Lake in April 1885 I continued on by stage to Dunseith. That spring and summer I built a sod house and a sod barn on the preemption and hired Karl Oslund to break five acres on the tree claim and Mr. Wulfer to break thirty acres on my preemption. Just before harvest I returned to St. Thomas. After the fall work was over that year I had a chance to go back to Rolette County with [a friend] who drove a yoke of oxen and a covered wagon. This time I brought with me my wife and young daughter Lizzie.

This time we stayed long enough to prove up on the preemption, which was fourteen months. Figuring the length of time from when I started improvements on it in April 1885, it would bring us up to about June 1886. As soon as I had proved up on it, I and my family again returned to St. Thomas. At this time I obtained work as section boss on the Great Northern Railroad between St. Thomas and Auburn. I held this job for six months during which time my wife worked out at whatever odd jobs she could get in St. Thomas. Our aim was to earn enough money to buy an outfit with which to work the farm. By the spring of 1887 our ambition had been realized. I then purchased a yoke of oxen, a wagon, and a plow at St. Thomas.

I came to start making improvements on the preemption. In Dunseith I had a friend whom I had known at St. Thomas. While I was building the sod shack, I stayed with him in Dunseith and walked back and forth night and morning; I thought nothing of walking the distance of approximately seven miles twice a day. After the shack was far enough advanced so I could sleep in it, I stayed there. The shack consisted of three rooms: a kitchen, a "parlor," and a bed room. The kitchen was eight feet wide and ten feet long, the "parlor" and the bedroom was each ten-feet square. They were arranged one after the other so that the shack was a long one, ten feet wide and twenty eight feet long. I covered my shack with poles, hay, and sod. In the center of the "parlor" I put up an oak post to help hold up the long roof which otherwise would have been too heavy for the walls. I plastered the walls inside and out and fastened a cloth under the ceiling to hold up the dirt and dust. There was a door to the west in the kitchen and one to the south in the "parlor." The house was built in an east and west direction. There were five half windows: two in the bed room, two in the "parlor," and one in the kitchen. In the "parlor" I put in a Turtle Mountain poplar lumber floor, but no floor either in the kitchen or bed room. I dug a

A Sod Homestead on the Plains

cellar under the "parlor." We lived in this house for about eight years. Kerosene was used for light and wood hauled gratis from the Turtle Mountains for fuel. I made a table and benches out of Turtle Mountain poplar lumber. I obtained groceries at Dunseith, hoofing it across the prairie with a sack on my back.

In addition to the sod shack I built a sod barn big enough for three oxen, one cow, and a team of horses. I dug a well in 1885. That was one of the requirements for holding and proving up on a preemption.

It took $250 to prove up on a preemption. I had no money when the time came to do that, so I borrowed that sum of $300. When the note and mortgage were due, I was yet short of money, so I told the mortgage company to take the land. The note then amounted to $350. The company told me that I had better try to hold the land, but I said that they had better take it over. And they did. Some time later I bought it back for $2,500, because my wife insisted on getting possession of it again.

In about 1900 I filed on a homestead in the same township in which were located my preemption and tree claim.

The Christian Colony Association

Charles Kono

ᔓhis could be a good chance to get a start in life.

Charles Kono (b. 1859) came to the United States in 1866 with his family from near Hamburg, Germany where his parents worked on a large farm. The Konoes settled near Ripon, Wisconsin, in a rural German community. After his father died in a runaway horse accident in 1869, he earned income for the family as a farm laborer. By 1880 he was earning two dollars a day. Like many who came to Dakota, Charles Kono joined a colony of like-minded people who jointly would seek and develop their farms.

I N THE FALL OF 1881 I HEARD OF A COLONY that was to be started in Dakota by the Christian Colony Association headed by Reverend Letts, W. W. Robinson and Major Bovay of Ripon, Wisconsin. This would be a good chance to get a start in life, so I got in touch with the colony board. In the spring of 1882 I paid the colony board twenty dollars for the right to join the colony and for transportation to Dakota Territory.

The colonists started from Ripon on the 20th of April 1882 and were supposed to pick up more members on the way so that there would be a special train of them (about three hundred) from St. Paul, Minnesota. It turned out that the board, especially Mr. Robinson, who was the most forceful of the board, had either misrepresented the facts or was mistaken, because there were only thirty people in the colony group when they left St. Paul.

The trip from St. Paul was very tedious as the Northern Pacific had just been built and the trains were very small and slow. When we arrived at Bismarck, we filled our satchels and what extra room we had in our trunks with food as there were no more towns west of Mandan where one could buy food. The train crossed the Missouri River at Bismarck by ferry, two coaches to a trip. At Mandan we saw proof of the high-water season of the Missouri River. There was nearly three feet of ice lying around the N.P. depot and practically all around the lower part of town. On about the 25th of April 1882 the colonists arrived at where Gladstone is now. It was a very dismal reception we got. An immigrant house, as the railroad company called it, was the only thing besides the rails that stood on a prairie blackened by fire the fall before. The thirty of us pilgrims, twenty-nine men and one woman, Mrs. Colonel Bissel of Waupon, Wisconsin, did not act nearly as enthusiastic as we should have on landing in the "land of plenty." The immigrant house was a shed about thirty by sixty feet divided by partitions into three rooms. The floor was dirt, and there were no furnishings. We tore boards from the snow fences to build bunks, and I found and cut some slough grass, which the fire had missed, for Mrs. Bissel to use as a mattress. I will never forget what the first night was like; it was cold, and I only had one horse blanket for myself and my partner to use for bedding.

Food was very hard to get, and no one was able to bring much along. We colonists were able to buy a limited amount of bread at the Green River section house which stood about three miles west of the present sight of Gladstone. Antelope were quite plentiful, so we were able to get meat quite easily. On the 3rd of May 1882 we colonists drew lots for claims. I had my claim about four miles east of Gladstone. We were quite disappointed in our leaders when they staked out the best claims for themselves before the drawing.

Reverend Cooke, pastor of the Methodist church at Mandan, held the first church services in the new colony on about May 20, 1882. The immigrant house was used for the place of worship as no church had been built.

The colony board owned a yoke of oxen and a walking plow which they rented to us colonists to plow the land. We had to do all of the work, care for and feed the animals; in addition the board charged us three dollars an acre for rental of the animals and plow. I planted potatoes for the first crop, and it turned out quite well. By autumn of 1882 the colony had grown to about eighty persons. Many of the colonists went back east for the winter as their houses were not very well-equipped.

My first house was a twelve- by sixteen-foot board shack with a dirt roof. It had two windows and one door and was furnished with a table, two chairs, a stove, and a bedstead. I had to rebuild this house twice as the wind blew it down once, and the second time it burned. My next home was eighteen by twenty-two feet and was shingled. I lived in this house until 1896 when I moved to Dickinson to take over the duties of sheriff of Stark County.

In the summer of 1882 the Northern Pacific Railroad Company built a depot and section house at Gladstone. Just before the depot was built, a lone immigrant from Nova Scotia came into the colony with a case of measles. It was not more than two weeks after his arrival, before we had a real epidemic of measles. Nearly every person in the colony had them. I had them pretty bad for two weeks and Mrs. Bissel cared for me.

I went to work for the Northern Pacific Railroad in the fall of 1882 in the track department and worked anywhere from Mandan to Missoula, Montana. Most of the work was caused by washouts. I quit the railroad in 1896 when I became sheriff. In 1896 when I moved to Dickinson and was elected sheriff of Stark County in a race with Jerry Hayes of Dickinson; it was the most spirited campaign I had ever experienced. Jerry even gave horses away to try to get votes, but I beat him by 112 votes, thanks to the help of Frank Lish, the former sheriff. The work was quite dead; only once in a while some cowboy would decide to hold a "six-shooter" celebration and would have to be jailed or chased home.

A German-Russian Homesteader

Jacob Kruckenberg

I had no furniture, and I slept on the floor on old sacks and rags.

The Kruckenberg family left Friedenstahl, southern Russia in 1888. Like many Germans they had been lured to the Black Sea area from Germany with the Russian promise of good land and exemption from military service. Jacob was seventeen in 1888 and gladly left Russia to escape the military draft which in the late nineteenth century was imposed on the Germans. Jacob relates the hardships that faced many German-Russians, many of whom settled the more arid region of North Dakota.

A T THAT TIME THE RUSSIAN GOVERNMENT drafted all young men when they became of age to serve a three years term in the army; the wage paid in the army was low, and the training was very hard work, and long hours, and the German soldiers in the Russian army were treated like animals and always got the hardest work to do, and some times even were fed separate from the real Russians with a very poor kind of food. Father filed [in Mercer County] in the late fall of 1888 but did not build until the midsummer of 1889. We stayed with the Ludwig Werner Sr. family the first year in Mercer County. I went to the western part of North Dakota and worked on a cattle ranch which was partly owned by a former president of the United States, Theodore Roosevelt. This ranch was located near Medora. I worked on that ranch for three years; they were running as high as three thousand head of cattle and about eight hundred head of horses. In the spring of 1892 I returned to Mercer county and helped father on the farm getting started farming. He and mother had two oxen and a hand plow which they bought from their neighbor for seventy-five dollars, and this was all they had to farm with. The seeding and all the cutting was done by hand. The first crop in 1889 was in fact the only crop they had up to 1895 on account of drought. From 1890 to 1895 the rains came too late for crops to mature, but there were good feed crops. The settlers picked buffalo bones and every other kind of bones for a living, hauled them to New Salem and Hebron, a distance of sixty-five miles. The trips were made with oxen and wagons and took ten days for a round trip. Bones sold from five to seven dollars per ton. What little money they had was spent for clothing, and food, and when they had more money than what they needed for food and clothing, it was saved to build a new lumber house, or barn, as the women did not like to live in the sod shanties without a floor or a piece of furniture.

In the year of 1890 they did not have one taste of meat for more than ten months; all they had to eat was milk, bread, and a few eggs about once a month. That was the hardest year they experienced. They were hungry and almost without clothes; no money to be made no matter how hard they tried.

In June 1895 I filed on a homestead which was one half mile south west of father's place. I built a one room sod shanty fourteen by twenty with three small windows; the roof was made from tree branches and dirt. The windows and lumber for the door were bought in Expansion, North Dakota which was an inland town on the Missouri River banks about eight miles north of the homestead. I had no furniture, and I slept on the floor on old sacks and rags. All I had was a cast-iron cook stove which was used for heating and cooking. I had two big wooden blocks: one was used for a chair and the other for a table. All I had to start farming was a hand plow and two old oxen. The grain and hay were cut with a hand sickle, worked together with forks, tied into bundles by hand, and hauled home on the farm place. In the fall of the year the grain was spread out on a level place and tramped on with oxen or horses until the kernel was out of the heads. Then the straw was removed with a fork. After the straw was removed the grain was shoveled back and forth on a windy day, and by doing that the wind blew the chaff away, and the grain was just as clean as if it had been threshed through a threshing machine.

On December 6, 1898 I married Emilia Wegerle of Mannhaven. A wedding dinner was served at the bride's parental home, and the afternoon was spent in visiting and singing. Only a few close friends were invited. The bride wore a blue dress with a white waist, while I wore a everyday blue work shirt and a new pair of common everyday blue trousers. The day after the wedding we went to our homestead shanty and slept on the floor, ate the meals on the wooden block the same as before. About a month later we bought some lumber and made a bedstead, a table, and two small benches. We were poor and picked bones for a living. The crops from 1895 to 1898 were good, but I did not have the equipment to put in much of a crop and therefore could not realize much. I always mined my own coal on father's homestead; the coal was easy to mine and was a good grade. The first well on the farm was dug by hand in 1895; the well was six by five and twenty-four-feet deep. This well was used for about twenty years and always had a big supply of water; the water was soft and clear and did not take much soap for washing clothes and also was a very good drinking water.

In 1901 I. P. Baker of Bismarck started to run boats on the Missouri River from Bismarck to Expansion. From then on all the farm produce was shipped by boat on the river to Bismarck where it was reloaded into railroad cars and shipped to eastern markets. All the necessities for the settlers were also shipped by boat from Bismarck to Expansion—such as lumber, machinery, clothing, flour, and groceries. Everything was cheap, and grain had a fair price; so we all got along well and were glad that we came to America. In the spring of 1902 I secured a job with Mr. Baker on one of the boats and worked for a period of three years for fifteen dollars per month and board. My wife stayed on the farm, raised a few chickens, and milked two cows and made a nice living for herself. I would come home about once a week for a day or so as long as the boat was in Expansion. In 1905 I quit the boat and went back to farming and cattle raising.

The town of Expansion was platted out in 1889 on the NE1/4 of section 27 147 86 in Mercer County on the Missouri River bank. This town grew fast and everyone in it was prosperous. At its highest peak in 1905 its population was 450 and had every kind of business needed

Steamboat on the Missouri at Bismarck
Because tracks on the other side were flooded, the railroad called on
the Benton Line for assistance in getting passengers across in the late
1880s, about the time Jacob Kruckenberg worked for I.P. Baker.

by the settlers. Farmers came as far as sixty miles from the west and forty miles from the south; the territory east only extended about eight miles to the river. Expansion had one of the largest farming territories in western North Dakota. Mr. P.S. Chaffee owned and operated the First State Bank of Expansion, which was opened for business in the spring of 1890; that bank at that time loaned as much as $2,000 on one quarter of land, on five- and ten-year terms, with a first mortgage on the land owned by the borrower, with interest at the rate of twelve percent.

From County Down to County Foster

Jennie Carrough Laughlin

♫t was a dreary sight indeed.

Born in County Down, Ireland, in 1862, Jennie Carrough migrated with her parents to America in 1880. She married Henry Laughlin, a Yankee-German, in 1881. The young couple was lured to the area around Carrington by the urgings of "Uncle Dodd." Their farming experience, as she relates it, represents a fairly typical profile of life on a Dakota homestead.

I N 1878 FATHER'S BROTHER HUGH, who had gone to America many years before, wrote that he was becoming blind and would like to have father come to America. Believing Hugh wished to be brought back to his old home in Ireland, he went at once as requested. Hugh Carrough had two quarters of land in America, one in Missouri and another in Iowa where he made his home. When father had been with him for some time, he found that Hugh did not wish to go back to Ireland but wished him to stay in America. His brother offered to give him the home quarter of land in Iowa (near Des Moines) if he would stay in America and let him stay with him. Father realized that there were far better opportunities in America and that he would be foolish to refuse his brother's generous offer and finally wrote mother to dispose of their property in Ireland and come to America and join him.

Mother wished me to accompany her and the other children to America, and this my grandmother wished her to do also. I disliked

75

leaving grandmother, but being a girl of seventeen years, I naturally wished to see more of the world. So, in the spring of 1880 mother and the children—Hugh, John, Minnie and Isabelle, and me (Jennie)—sailed.

Mother was loathe to leave her mother and her home since birth but knew her place was with her husband. However, she was never completely happy in the United States. I also felt bad at leaving my grandmother, whom I never saw again as she died some two or three years later.

We left Ireland from Lorn, embarking on the steamship *Indiana*. The trip was fairly rough, and many of the passengers were ill. However, I loved every minute of it, as I loved the ocean. We traveled second cabin which made it more comfortable than for those who were below. The food was frugal and poorly cooked, and the boat was old and slow. We landed in New York harbor, fourteen days after leaving Ireland. This was the last voyage of the *Indiana* as it was condemned for further use.

The railroad journey took three days and nights from New York to Altoona, Iowa. This was some six miles from our destination, the farm where we were to make our future home. Mother and the two smaller children, four and six years old, walked the six miles and left the older children with father's sister who lived in Stuart, Iowa.

We found life somewhat different in America from what we were familiar with. The farms were much larger. We now had a hundred-sixty acre farm compared to the thirty-five acres in Ireland.

Early in the spring Henry Laughlin came to work in Iowa when he was about twenty-three years old, and there met me. We were married at the home of my parents on December 22, 1881 by the Lutheran minister from a nearby town. We then rented a farm in that same locality and began married life.

On January 15, 1883 our son Francis Dodd Laughlin was born. He was named for my dearly loved uncle Francis Dodd. A month or so later Uncle Francis Dodd gave us a most pleasant surprise when he stopped to see us; the first time I had seen him since he left Ireland in 1871, although we corresponded. He told us that he had left his wife and daughter in Colorado and was on his way to Dakota to take up land;

they were to follow when he had made the necessary arrangements. He urged us to also take up land in Dakota, and we were greatly tempted as we were only renting where we were, and I did not like the idea of having to move every so often. However, we felt that we could not decide on such short notice and asked Uncle Francis to write us of the country and opportunities when he had been there for a while. This he did, telling us of the vast prairies in their original primitive state; that there were few settlers in the country as yet, but that there were great opportunities for young persons to obtain land with little money. He told us to use our own judgment in coming to Dakota as there were great hardships to be borne, much hard work to be done and loneliness; and he did not want us to be unhappy and disappointed and blame him in any way. We delayed any decision that year but kept thinking of it.

The next summer of 1884 we again heard from Uncle Dodd that settlers were arriving steadily and that he was fond of the new country. He had settled in the southwestern part of Foster County near the long range of hills later called the Hawk's Nest. The township he had named Pleasant Valley for the surrounding hills and the beautiful sunsets and distances to be seen.

Later that summer we disposed of all of our furniture and stock and toward the middle of November boarded the train for Dakota. We took only personal belongings and sent a large box containing high chair, sewing machine, kitchen utensils, dishes, and bedding.

The trip from Des Moines to Carrington took two days and nights and meant two changes of trains. On November 17, 1884, we arrived in Carrington via the Northern Pacific branch from Jamestown. Francis Dodd was there to meet us and took us to his small homestead of two tiny rooms where we spent the first two months until we could secure land and a home of our own.

My first impression on alighting from the train was that I could see every house in town and not a tree. It was a dreary sight indeed at that time of the year, particularly for one used to the luxuriant growth of Ireland and the woods and orchards of Iowa.

We stayed with the Dodds until the first part of January 1885. Shortly after our arrival Henry filed on a quarter of land located in the same township in which the Dodds were living, and he and Mr. Dodd began immediately the building of a one-room house.

The small claim house was built in December and January under great difficulties as that was a winter of severe cold and great snow storms. The house was built of shiplap which was hauled from Carrington; this Uncle Dodd did as Henry had no way of securing it himself. The house was built very simply with one door and only one window because we could not put in another one that year. On the inside it was lined with card board because we could not afford tar paper or other sealing materials. The one room was fourteen by sixteen and was used without being added on to for seven or eight years. In January of 1885 we moved into our new home.

We now realized the terrible mistake we had made in selling all of our furniture, farm implements, and stock before coming to Dakota. We had sold at a loss, not knowing that things were expensive and also difficult to secure in Dakota. We had practically nothing to begin with and little money left from our railroad fare and building the house. We bought a four-lid cook stove which was used for heating purposes and a bedstead. Henry then made a table and some straight chairs. He also made a trundle bed for the baby which could be slid under the larger bed in the daytime. Later he made a couch which we had for many years. On February 24, 1885 a second son, John, was born in the small, roughly built claim shack.

That winter was indeed a hard one. It was very cold and we were never really warm. There was never much to eat in the house. Uncle Dodd would bring something occasionally and would ask if we had flour. Being proud I would never admit the real circumstances, but a day or so later a bag of flour would be brought to us. Occasionally we would buy a little tea and that was really the extent of the provisions, except for milk.

A neighbor, John Hallberg, had come to Dakota two years before from Minnesota and settled first in Stutsman County in the spring of 1882. Then later in the spring of 1883 he came to Foster County. He saw our plight of having two babies to care for and little to do with. That winter of 1884-85 he walked from his own home to ours (a mile or so) in severe weather and when the snow was three feet or more deep to bring milk for the babies. His kindness was never forgotten.

We did not leave home that winter except for a few visits to the Dodds; also a few times Henry was given a ride into town to secure provisions and the mail. The mail was irregular as the train would not be brought through for weeks at a time due to the great snow drifts. Whenever I would receive a letter from mother, I would be overjoyed to find a dollar bill tucked into it, which meant warmth and food for the little ones. I did not go into Carrington for several years after arriving in Foster County and then it would always be two or three years between trips. Our farm was located on the northern edge of Pleasant Valley Township, some five or six miles from Carrington.

In the spring of 1885 everything seemed more hopeful with warmth in the air and the prairies turning green. Through the spring and summer Henry hired twenty acres of his land broken as he had no horses or farm implements with which to do the work himself. We had little money to hire much done, either, so it was some years before we could farm in a very large way. I planted a garden on the breaking, and it did very well. The vegetables did not mature as they did later on well cultivated ground, but they did better than expected. The potatoes particularly were very good on the breaking. Most successful were the hardier vegetables such as cabbage, lettuce, onions, parsnips, radishes, carrots, and other root vegetables as that was a cool, wet summer. I also planted pie plant roots sent by a friend in Iowa and this grew wonderfully.

That spring Mr. Hallberg again came to our aid. He knew we must have milk for the children and that we had no money with which to buy cows. He offered us a Hereford cow for $50, to be paid for when we could do so and no hurry. He did not particularly care whether we paid for the cow or not, but he did know that we were proud and he must be tactful. We were indeed grateful to him; if it had not been for John Hallberg, we did not know how we would ever have made a start. In the fall the cow was giving no more milk and Mr. Hallberg offered us another fresh cow for $35 on the same basis. These two cows were the beginning of the large herd of cattle of later years; all of the cattle came from these two, and it was many years before they were paid for. There was then plenty of milk for the babies, and also we could have a little butter.

During that summer Henry built a sod barn large enough for the cows and their offspring. This barn was used for about ten years and was enlarged when necessary. That summer of 1885 Francis Dodd gave me two or three hens, and I raised ten chickens from them. We felt very well off that fall with potatoes for the winter, two cows, and ten chickens. However, one great disappointment was in securing water. The water in the well on the homestead was poor, and we hauled most of the water for the house from springs and wells on other farms.

That summer we saw Indians for the first time. We were in fear of them, having heard many wild Indian stories when living in the more eastern states. The trail from Fort Totten to the Standing Rock reservation ran through our land, and the Indians did not change their course because of inhabitants. They would often stop and ask for food and drink which I never refused because I hoped to be rid of them the sooner. However mean looking they might be, they did not steal or molest anything through all of the years.

One day in the later summer of 1885 we had just finished the noon meal when Henry went to the window and pointed out that there were two Indians riding toward the house from the north with guns over their shoulders. I told him to stay in the house until the Indians were by, and we watched them ride up to the house. Henry then went outside to waylay them; they held out their hands in a friendly way and then asked in their sign language for food. They stood their guns up against the house and followed Henry inside where he asked me to feed them. I set the table with dishes and silverware and was glad that I still had a kettle of cabbage and another of potatoes on the stove, and also had plenty of bread in the house. After I had put the food on in serving dishes, Henry told the Indians that they might sit down at the table. They completely ignored the plates and silverware before them and ate out of the serving dishes; one would eat by handfuls from the cabbage and the other from the potatoes, and then they would exchange. The bread disappeared like magic; I kept replenishing the bread plate and all would go. Finally when I had given them almost three loaves of bread, I decided I would watch and see if they were actually eating it; two men could never consume that much food. I then saw that they would empty the plate and tuck the slices of bread into their blankets, so I decided that I would offer them no more or there would be nothing left for ourselves. I was chagrined that I had given them as much as I had, only to have it stored away in their blankets for future use. When they had finished their meal, we breathed a sign of relief, but in vain. They went over to the stove and sat down and drew out their pipes with stems a foot and a half long. They smoked contentedly, every so often offering a pipe to Henry who could never smoke without becoming ill. He finally made them understand that he could never smoke, and they seemed reconciled and soon took their leave. This had also been their way of offering thanks for the meal and being friendly. I afterwards berated Henry for not smoking as they might have become angry. These two Indians had not been gone for more than fifteen or twenty minutes when a lone Indian rode into the yard and up to the house. He was dressed in a sort of uniform, navy blue with brass buttons. He told us partly by speaking and partly by sign language that he wished food. There was nothing left from dinner for him, but I gave him bread, butter, and tea and he seemed to appreciate it. He ate with the manners of a white man, using the plates and silverware as they were supposed to be used. When he had finished he thanked us and asked about the two men who had preceded him; then he was also on his way without wasting any time.

The Indians usually had ponies which the men rode; sometimes they would have wagons or buggies. The women, however, always walked unless they were very aged or ill. Often they would carry small children or provisions. The men always rode if there were horses to ride.

In the spring of 1886 Henry put into crop the twenty acres of land which had been broken the previous year; he put two or three acres into oats and the balance into wheat. We purchased a team of oxen and a second hand plow in the summer, but oxen cannot work in warm weather, so Henry was able to break only about ten or fifteen acres more of land that year. Sometimes I would hitch up the oxen to the hay rack in those next few summers and go to spend the day with a friend or neighbor.

Our small crop of that first year was very good. The wheat went about thirty bushels to the acre with a good price. This gave us a little money for the winter's provisions. The seed wheat we would clean with a fanning mill which worked by hand and which was lent back and forth among neighbors. We had practically no corn in the early years; it was very hard to grow. At first we had what they called "squaw corn"—short ears and poorly matured. The first sweet corn we had was a real pleasure, and then there was scarcely enough for many meals. We shelled the seed corn out by hand, the little we had.

In the spring of 1886 the schoolhouse was built on the banks of the Pipestem Creek. Mr. J.M. Ruth, who taught for two years, spent much of his spare time at our home. He had an enrollment of some twenty pupils.

Sometimes I would hitch up the oxen and hayrack, load in the children, and go to Wyard Township to visit John Pre, a bachelor who was working a claim there. He was from County Down, Ireland, also. He was somewhat older than I, but he used to give me a lift to school occasionally in the old country. We had much in common and loved to talk of the old country. Later his nephew, Henry Garret, also from Ireland, came to stay with him and then took a claim.

On October 24, 1886, a daughter, Mary Elizabeth, was born, so we then had three small children to feed and keep clothed. Occasionally my mother would send me material or clothes to make over, and I would then have a regular orgy of sewing, which I loved to do. We had no money with which to buy clothes or materials, but I made nearly everything. The overalls I made even when the boys were grown to men, as they preferred them to those they could buy. I would also knit mittens, caps, and socks when I had the material with which to work. The men's clothing for Henry was mostly purchased at the general stores in Carrington.

Each year was much the same as that preceding it. A little more land would be broken, and a little more crop planted each year. The crops were nearly always good in those early years. There was plenty of snow and average rain, and cool summers benefited the crops. It was considered average to have twenty or twenty-five bushels of wheat to the acre, and in boom years there would be around thirty bushels and even more to the acre.

In 1888 there was much cold weather during the summer with occasional frosts and an early freeze before the grain was matured to

Shocking Grain in Dakota

cut. This caused poor grain and dark, sticky flour. In 1889 and 1890 there was no rain or snow to speak of which caused crop failures in most parts. However, there was the Pipestem River and many large sloughs in that part of the county, and the people did not suffer as much from the freeze and drought as those in the eastern part of the country. Crops were always fair in spite of these things.

In 1888 we bought three horses, and the farm work progressed more rapidly; we were able to put more land into crop. Shortly after that we purchased 240 acres of land from Mr. Sykes of the Sykes-Hughes Land Company, an English concern which had large tracts of land in western Foster County and in Wells County. We paid about seven dollars an acre for the land. Many of the settlers were able to buy up preemptions where the original filer of the land had deserted; this land could be purchased reasonably. However, we were not able to do this because we had no money to invest at the time. Later we also purchased a quarter which joined our homestead.

One year in about 1891 we came to Carrington for a Fourth of July celebration. It was a cold day so we wore our heavy clothing; during the day snow fell.

The best crop of the early years was in 1891. The crops for the most part ran from thirty-five to forty bushels of wheat to the acre and had seventy bushels of oats to the acre. There was also a good price that year because the three preceding years had been almost complete failures for most of the country.

Life On The Homestead

Paulina Schlueter

'Lhe prairie was just a vast sea of tall grasses.

Pauline Schlueter was born in 1869 at Iron Ridge, Wisconsin, where her father, a native of Germany, was a foreman in the mines who earned good wages. In 1870 August Beling, a fellow mine worker, convinced Schlueter to join him in seeking a new home in Dakota. Although Paulina Schlueter was just a toddler when her parents struck out for Richland County, she has put together a vivid story of everyday homestead life in the 1870s and 1880s through her own recollections and those that were passed down to her.

In 1889 Paulina married William Clark, who had quit his job at a foundry in Red Wing, Minnesota, and accompanied his parents to Richland County in 1882 at age nineteen. For two years they lived in a tarpaper shack on their homestead. Their first child was born dead in 1890, but they had six other children, including a set of twins, between 1891 and 1897.

HE PARTY OF THREE COVERED WAGONS drawn by a team of two horses set out in the early morning of a bright fall morning. The wagons were packed to overflowing with furniture, bedding, clothing, food, and feed for the teams. Behind each wagon a crate was tied which carried chickens and ducks. The older children drove a small herd of cattle, most of which belonged to us. The trip took three long weeks of rough hard driving. In September we reached Dakota. At Breckenridge, Minnesota, the last town to the west, we stopped there for two days for resting, getting direction, and laying in a supply of food.

There was not a bridge across the river, so we drove the teams through the river. Then the herd of stock was driven through, and our party bade farewell to civilization and set our eyes to searching the vast prairie for a sight of some living humans. We didn't pass a house along the way and didn't see a living soul until about noon when we saw a man in the field to the left.

When we reached the river, the horses needed watering, so the men took them to the river and the children followed, and they found the ground covered with plums. While the men were away, mother grew hysterical and cried and screamed and laughed. She cried and cried and begged father to return to the east where we had come from. She even told him she would go back alone if he didn't get me out of such a land. After several weeks on the prairie she became more herself and began to like the life as well as my father did. Mrs. Beling wished to return, but she didn't even ask to leave because she knew that her husband didn't have enough money to make such a trip.

The women and young children were left in the wagons while the men and older children decided upon the land. Father homesteaded in Richland County. The sod home was put up in this fashion: a hole three feet was dug about ten by twelve feet; over this, poles were placed crosswise over two upright poles. This made the foundation for the roof which was covered with branches; then chunks of sod were laid on top of that to keep the wind from tearing the branches off. The sides above the three-foot hole were sodded up, and the home was completed in a short time. The family lived in this and in the covered wagon until the new log home was completed, our first permanent home on the prairie. It was a twelve- by fourteen-foot main structure with two lean-tos: one on the north, seven- by fourteen-feet, and one on the west which served as the barn. The logs were all hand-cut and plastered together to fill in the crack between the logs with mud mixed with straw and slough grass. The interior was smoothed off as well as it could be, and one coat of white wash was given it the first spring. The roof was made from split logs covered with sod for warmth. This log house and barn were used for over ten years.

The barn had not been as well-built. In the winter of 1874 father expected a newborn calf, and he sat many nights keeping track of the cow so that he would be at hand to care for the calf when it came so it wouldn't get chilled; even a new calf meant much to us. He had sat up the most of three nights in January, and on the fourth night he decided to sleep a little because it seemed warmer, and he felt sure he would hear any disturbance in the barn. He was so tired that he fell into a sound sleep, and when he did awaken, he heard the calf bellowing. He rushed into the cold barn only to find the new-born calf with a frozen tail and frosted ears.

In 1876 we got our first hog. Father bought it from someone in Elizabeth, Minnesota, and about a month later we children went to the hog barn, a small sod protection, and found eight pink and white pigs. We were so tickled at the find that we gathered the white animals up and rushed to the house screaming with delight at all the little animals we had found. We didn't know what they were but thought we had found some animal that we could keep for pets.

That fall we were sent to gather acorns for the hog—the choice ones were to be saved out for coffee substitute. We gathered the acorns which were plentiful on the river bank. We grew tired of gathering them, so we decided to rest, and while we rested we climbed up into some of the trees. One of us discovered one tree which had a large hollow branch, and in this hollow we found a supply of the choice acorns which the squirrels had gathered for their winter eating. We decided to take the acorns and go home with the lovely supply. We took about half of the acorns from the tree, and then decided that we hadn't better steal any more because we would leave the squirrels without any food for the winter. The next year we did the same thing, only we took the choice acorns and left in their place the smaller ones which had been left on the ground. These acorns were roasted in a slow oven until brown then the outer covering was taken off; the nut itself was then ground for coffee. This drink didn't taste like coffee, but it gave the hot water a flavor and seemed to be more satisfying than just hot water for a meal.

We did all of the family sewing by hand in the home. Mother did it all until the daughters were old enough to be taught how. She made dresses from dark brown and blue denim; each girl had only one new dress a season, and the dress from the season before was used as second dress when a new one was made if the girl had not out grown it. The little girls wore aprons of bright prints to cover their dark dresses. The aprons were washed with the weekly wash, but the dresses were washed only every four or five weeks at the most. The men and boys handed down their trousers and shirts when they outgrew them. The work clothes for the men were many times made from sacks and shirts of denim. They wore heavy shoes and home-knitted socks. The underwear was made from red or blue flannel. The girls underskirts were many yards of flannel gathered on to a belt at the waistline, and for Sundays these dark flannel skirts were covered with white full skirts with yards of lace at the hem.

Though we never suffered from the lack of money with which to buy food, we many times went to bed hungry because the weather was bad and the men folks in the neighborhood wouldn't dare to set out on the trail to go to town for supplies. We learned to pick out the good berries which grew along the river and also soon learned to pull the weed which has many roots and at the end of each root a sort of potato formed. These so called wild potatoes were sweet in their taste, and we liked to eat them raw. And after eating the raw berries and other things which we found in the woods, we would return home for the evening meal not hungry for more than a light lunch.

Mrs. Beling would come to our home in the spring and make pounds of soft and hard soap for us. She then would come to our home again in the fall and cook—out-of-doors on an open fire in the big soap kettle—plums for jams. This plum butter and jam was stored in large open crocks for the winter use. The sap of the box elder tree was taken and cooked down to a thick syrup which had a sort of sweet-bitter taste. This was called sugar water and used on bread for lunches. We used many pounds of beans during the winters. These beans were soaked then boiled for soup, to which the fat or dripping from the meat was added for flavoring. Many times the beans were boiled and then placed in the oven and baked two or three days. In the dish of beans, which were to be baked, small chunks of fat pork or smoked meat were added and molasses added for coloring.

During the long evenings the room was lighted by bright kerosene lamps or even candles, but only on very rare occasions. We always had a supply of kerosene on hand, but it was used as a medicine. When one

An Early Dakota Homestead
The "flag" on the right was a clock to tell the worker in the field the time to come in for dinner.

of the family was taken sick with a cold or stomach pains, a spoon of kerosene was given them, and they soon were up and around again. We hated the sight of the kerosene, but it helped us and was one of the remedies used by all families. I learned to gather a fern-like weed and save the blossom. This blossom when dried would keep for years and was very good medicine for stomach ache and diarrhea. It was called sheep's gall and was very bitter tea to take.

The prairie was just a vast sea of tall grasses. It was possible to see for miles. There were no trees on the prairie except along the river where there was a growth of trees and underbrush. To the south and west one could see the outline of the blue hills which were near the reservation in the southern part of the Dakota Territory. There were no towns or villages to obstruct the view, nor were houses and barns to be seen above the prairie grass.

Four Young Women Homesteaders

Sally and Mary Troska, Helen and Christina Sonnek

An idea struck me. What fun it would be.

Four young women in their late teens and early twenties made a momentous decision in 1900. The four would go to North Dakota and homestead adjacent quarter sections. It was all Clara "Sally" Troska's idea, but the other three entered the bold adventure wholeheartedly. Sally, who was not yet nineteen years old, tells one of North Dakota's most amazing homestead tales. After she proved up on her homestead, she went to Minneapolis where she worked in a millinery works. In 1907 she married E. W. Eaton and returned to her farm. But drought and crop failures forced the Eatons off the land in 1913. They returned to Minnesota.

Sally Troska

I WAS SECOND TO THE YOUNGEST of a family of twelve children, all raised on a beautiful farm in Faribault County, Minnesota. My father died seven years before mother's death. We all stayed on the farm until the youngest reached the age of twenty-one. My brother did not want to farm, so we all were leaving because the old homestead was rented. At this time I intended to take a complete course at a business college. But at that time many people were getting interested in the North Dakota land boom which greatly interested my oldest sister and a cousin. I listened to their plans. I decided I could homestead and make a fourteen-month proof, then go to business college. An idea struck me, what fun it would be. So I rode a horse to the home of my cousin, a girl of my own age, and told her of my latest—what I thought to be a wonderful plan. Her widowed mother was horrified at the idea of going to the farthest corner of North Dakota and the risk of being harmed by the Indians. The idea of making the venture and getting a real thrill appealed to Chris, but she felt that she should ask her oldest brother. So she took a horse and we both rode out to where her brother Peter was harvesting. He had a good hearty laugh; then he gave his consent and handed her the cream check of a little over $65. Then right away there were many busy hands packing the luggage and making lunches for the trip. We worked fast and were soon enroute for North Dakota: myself (Sally by nickname), my older sister [Mary], Cousin Chris, and an older cousin [Helen]. Chris took her little rifle strapped on outside of her suitcase—the end of the barrel just happened to be projecting slightly into the aisle of the coach which we boarded. Pretty soon a lady walking down the aisle caught her dress on end of rifle barrel which resulted in quite a large tear. We apologized and immediately rearranged the suitcase.

When we arrived at St. Paul, we secured landseekers' tickets at greatly reduced rates. Every coach on the train of many coaches was just packed with people, mostly emigrants, but many were laborers on the way to the Dakota harvest fields. Arriving at Minot, the crowd was so large that all could not make much headway by staying on the sidewalk, so we and many others followed the street, which then looked more like just a road. Minot was a railroad division point of the Great Northern. The main line of the Soo also ran through Minot, and the land office also was located there. Many who wished to sell relinquishment on their claims crowded around all of these newcomers, so we soon had plenty of information on every part of that whole district. Bowbells seemed to appeal to us as being the best place to go and look around; so after staying a day and night at Minot, we went on to Bowbells, arriving rather late in the afternoon. We were directed to a hotel. Chris and I each carried our mandolins, so we gave the people there the impression we were a show troupe. The next day we engaged a livery man to take us on a land hunting tour. For many miles out, the land had been broken up and was into crops. There were no graded roads—just trails that went corner ways across every school section. At about twelve miles southwest we came to a range of hills; then the trail was very winding out to where there was still some claims that had not been filed on. During this ride in the hills we only passed one residence, a sod house.

None of us had much idea about how to select good farming land, except my oldest cousin. She had remembered her father saying that when anyone goes into a new territory looking for desirable land, one should take along a spade and dig down at several places on each tract of land. We four girls wanted to file on a square section. But by doing so, we all would not have good land, so two of us filed on one half-section and the other two on half of another section. These two halves cornered each other. In this way we all could not have our shacks close to each other. But we arranged so that two of us could be near to each other, also the other two could be near together, a mile from us. The oldest cousin built the best and largest shack, one which would be comfortable in winter. She bought a kitchen range. The rest of us did our baking at her place. We three each had a two-griddle stove, commonly called laundry stove. We could nicely fry our meat, potatoes, etc. and also boil water to do our washings. We each lived in our own shack during pretty cold winter weather. We each had a well that furnished sufficient water.

Each of us also had twelve acres of land broke up and put into crops. We had several furrows plowed around and out a short distance from each shack which we called firebreaks. The price we paid for doing the plowing was two dollars and fifty cents per acre. During the warm weather the hills were beautiful; there were many different varieties of wild flowers on the hillsides and in the coulees between the hills. June berries were plentiful, and we used them for sauce, pies, and jam. Between the hills were many ponds of water usually called pot holes by the few ranchers who lived in this range of hills. In the pot holes wild ducks were in abundant numbers each season until ice began to form on the water. Chris made good use of her little rifle, and we often had duck meat to eat. During the autumn months we had several visitors who were men with guns and dogs. They would shoot ducks and prairie chickens in large numbers, but they never could seem to get all of them.

There always seemed to be plenty of game fowls. Many droves of cattle were driven through. The drivers on horseback were called cowboys. None of them had the rough appearance that we sometimes read about cowboys. We let them herd the cattle on our grass. None of them knew a thing about milking, but they would let us milk the gentle cows; and then we would have good cream and cottage cheese. All of these cowboys were fully as gentlemanly and neat in appearance as any men we ever knew. We could get our mail and groceries at the foot hill, a distance of twelve miles. So we decided to buy a horse and a buggy. After doing this we were able to go more often, and then we got our mail mostly once a week, always within ten days. If we had too large and heavy a load of supplies, only one of us would go as the trail was rough, and many of the hills were so steep that it was burdensome for one horse to pull. We could get good lignite coal at the foot hills for $2.50 per ton. The price delivered was twenty dollars per ton.

We got established on our claims in April 1906. We planned on making a fourteen-month proof. While we were not on our claims, we had steady work in Bowbells. So many restaurants and hotels meant a demand for many waitresses. Although we had no previous experience in this line of work, we soon learned to do such work. The money we earned enabled us to buy supplies needed on the claims. We soon had many friends who would come out to our claims and hunt. We have dressed and roasted enough ducks in one day to feed a party numbering over thirty. Whenever they happened to stay over night, we arranged to have them sleep at the shacks of some of our men neighbors. Hay would be brought in and laid on the floors, then blankets spread over the hay. This enabled the hunters to be at the best hunting grounds at early daybreak. Before starting out, they would gather up all of the hay and feed to the horses picketed near by. The girl friends that came along would double up with us girls that had claim shacks. We always had cots enough to give them a comfortable place to sleep.

The winters of 1905 and 1906 were both plenty severe. There were quite a large number of blizzards. One day in October had been mild all day, and my sister and I thought we would go out to the claims. So a man employed at the livery barn was engaged to take us out. He went by the name of Old Steve. He was quite old. We had quite a large supply of things to take. Steve was slow about getting started, and we didn't leave Bowbells until two, or about three. About halfway out as we were getting near the hills, snow began to fall; then very soon it got dark. By this time it was snowing real hard. We had never experienced a real blizzard so we were not scared, but we noticed that Old Steve acted nervous. We felt confident that he knew the hills. After awhile he stopped the horses, and he got out and looked around. By now it was completely dark. None of us could even see out as far as one inch. And now we fully realized that we were lost.

We went ahead until the horses stopped. Then we all got out and found that the horses were against a wire fence. This pleased Old Steve. He broke the fence down and drove inside. He said we will find that someone lives within this enclosure. After driving on a little farther, he noticed a light. We come to a sod house. The light Steve had noticed was a lantern carried by two men who also were lost, and they arrived at the sod house just ahead of us. The house had only two rooms. The family numbered eight. But they all seemed pleased to give us shelter. The storm raged on. We all stayed there four nights and three days. The lady had lots of yarn on hand, so my sister and I made caps and mittens for the children. They had a plentiful supply of fuel, potatoes, milk, etc. Two of their beds were made of bed springs that they swung up against the walls during day-time; they also had a few cots. All of the men slept on the floor. The morning after the fourth night was clear, so we soon got out to our claims. The drifts were hard enough most of the way to hold up the horses, but they broke through a few times. We drove on and on; finally, we sighted cousin Helen's shack. Smoke was coming out of the stove pipe on top, so we knew she must be safe. She heard us drive up, so she opened a window to admit us. A big drift had the door completely covered. No one had suffered at all, so we all felt very thankful. Another blizzard caught us all out there in the following November. Chris and I were together. Because the snow was so deep we hadn't tried to go to where Mary and Helen were, and the sky was looking plenty threatening. Presently we saw a team approaching at a high rate of speed. As it drew near we noticed the horses were hitched to a half-sleigh. The sleigh had no tongue so sometimes it would slide around and almost in front of the horses.

A Homestead Sod Shack in Winter

Soon the man yelled, "Get your things and come with me, there is a blizzard coming, cannot tell how long it will last." Well, we just did as he bade. Soon we were on the sleigh, hanging on for dear life. It was great fun. We arrived at a shack sixteen- by twenty-feet. A dear old lady eighty-two years of age welcomed us. She was the mother of three bachelor sons who were with her. All were homesteading. This old mother's hair was burned off of her head from the result of putting kerosene in the boiler with soap.

The men got busy getting in coal and water and stretching a rope from house to barn to be used as a guide. We got supper. They had plenty of fresh meat, just freshly butchered—a beef. The storm continued and it grew colder. No one dared venture out. We played cards, then retired. There were two beds. The mother and oldest son occupied one; Chris and I the other. The other two brothers made up their bed on the floor. We had to stay here four days as the blizzard continued. We baked cookies and more cookies. I remember we made seven mince meat pies and doughnuts, and we baked bread as it was hard for mother

Palmer to bake. After the blizzard cleared, Dan took the same rig and took us to where my sister and cousin lived in their shacks. They were O.K. We stayed with them a few days then went to our shacks.

Our day for proving up was to be the 26th day of December. We waited for Old Steve to come and get us. We expected him one day, so we planned to start back the next day with bag and baggage. He was delayed on account of the snow. We were low on supplies. At three o'clock there was no Steve, so we knew we weren't going to Bowbells that day. Then we decided to make some candy. We jokingly mentioned that the "Prince of the stories did not happen to find us in the hills." We looked out and noticed far away some person was walking. We couldn't imagine who would venture out alone, on foot in such deep snow. We finished making candy and then looked out again. Lo and behold, a man was coming towards our shack. As he drew near, we watched through the window. This was the first time out there that we had felt frightened. He wore high boots, his cap was pulled down over his ears. He was very large and husky, his face heavily bearded. The thought struck me—"Jesse James." He wore a belt with four revolvers. He rapped loud and boldly at the door. We opened the door, and he stepped right in and sat down. We sure were frightened. We offered him something to eat, including candy, which he accepted. He took notice of everything. He took down our little rifle and examined it. Then he drew one of his revolvers and handed it to me remarking, "Isn't this a dandy." We didn't know what to expect. After keeping us in this suspense for one and a half hours, he decided to go. On leaving he remarked, "If I get a rabbit, I will return and give it to you." We were afraid to stay, but on account of the deep snow we knew we could not get to any of the other shacks. So we barred our door and hung a blanket over the window so that no light would guide him back if he decided to return. This was our last night on the claims. Our driver came in the morning and we went to Bowbells. And we and our witnesses boarded the midnight flyer and went to Minot to prove up. We all got a clear title to our claim without any trouble. My deed was signed by President Theodore Roosevelt.

Index

About the editors . . .

Historian D. Jerome Tweton returned to his hometown, Grand Forks, North Dakota, to teach in the University of North Dakota history department in 1965 after receiving his Ph.D. from the University of Oklahoma. For most of his thirty-year tenure at the University, he served as department chairman. Tweton's books include The Marquis de Morès: Dakota Capitalist, French Nationalist and The New Deal at the Grassroots: Programs for the People in Otter Tail County, Minnesota. A senior consultant to the North Dakota state partner of the National Endowment for the Humanities, Tweton has written and edited books and articles about the history of North Dakota for citizens of all ages, including text books and instructional material for classroom use. In addition to his work as an academic historian who has edited publications, written seven books and scores of articles, Tweton has participated in over 300 public humanities programs in North Dakota and throughout the nation. He and his wife Paula own and operate a bed-and-breakfast in a renovated turn-of-the-century home which is on the National Register of Historic Places, the Beiseker Mansion in Fessenden, North Dakota.

Everett C. Albers has served as the executive director of The North Dakota Humanities Council, the state partner of the National Endowment for the Humanities, since it began in 1973. Albers is one of the founders of the modern Chautauqua movement which features first-person characterizations of historical writers and thinkers presented in tents during summer tours of the Great Plains. He holds an M.A. in English from Colorado State University and has taught humanities and English. A North Dakota native who grew up on a family homestead in Oliver County, Albers lives with his wife Leslie in Bismarck. They are the parents of Albert and Gretchen. Albers operates Otto Design, a desktop publishing concern, and the publishing house Northern Lights, ND Press, as an avocation. He co-edited The Legacy of North Dakota Country Schools and the 1998 Behold Our New Century: Early 20th Century Visions of America and has written several children's coloring books featuring Seaman, the dog who went with Lewis and Clark, as well as the 2002 The Saga of Seaman: The Story of the Dog Who Went with Lewis & Clark.